Together

Making Your Marriage Work
from the Start

Together

Making Your Marriage Work from the Start

Debra Washington Gould
and
Joseph Gould Jr.

 **BookPartners**
Wilsonville, Oregon

DEDICATION

To our parents, Joseph Gould Sr., Gloria Madison Washington and Herman Emanuel Washington Sr., whom we love so much. The positive images you projected into our lives during our early years truly made a difference. You inspired and encouraged us and taught us never to give up.

This book is dedicated to the memory of Joe's mother, Fannie Raphael Gould, who loved, supported, motivated and encouraged us up until her death, and who inspires us to this day. We will love you always!

To Debra's late grandparents, Edward and Viola Madison. Your love, your giving and your wisdom will always be remembered.

To all of our aunts, uncles, brothers, sisters and cousins. Thanks for being family. Special thanks to Debra's sister Lynda Washington; her Aunt Geraldine Madison, Aunt Betty Madison Cummings and Aunt Lillie Mae Madison. You have given Debra much more than she will ever be able to return. Debra sends special love and appreciation to her sister-in-law Pamela Grant Sherrard. "We are together because you introduced me to your wonderful brother."

To our friend and mentor Thelma L. Wells, a gracious thank you for contributing so much love and support to our lives and for your thoughtful message in the Foreword.

To our beautiful son, Joseph Gould III. You are the greatest gift and God has blessed us with so much love, joy and happiness through you. ♥

Contents

Foreword

Living "happily ever after" is an expectation that
many people (particularly women) bring to marriage. I
know I did. That is, until the first week after my wedding.
All of a sudden, things were not as perfect as I had
dreamed. It seemed that George and I had more disagreements during that first week than we had had during
the previous six years of courtship. I thought he was being
bossier. He thought I was grouchier. I think both of us
wondered what we had gotten ourselves into. Perhaps you
have experienced the same feelings at one time or another
in your marriage relationship. I'm happy to report,
however, that I've been married to the same man for more
than thirty-seven years. Things do get better. Hallelujah!

Things get better, but they don't get better by themselves. You cannot simply leave your relationship alone
and expect it to improve. You must put in effort before you
will see success. This book is about investing energy,
enthusiasm, expectations, empathy, efficient organization,
effective communication, enlightenment, entertainment,
education, endearment, excitement and ecstasy into your
marriage relationship to yield the highest benefits—for
you, your children, and for generations to come.

Writing from the perspective of their twenty-three
years of marriage, Joe and Debra Gould offer information,

inspiration, encouragement and motivation to help you understand how working *together* provides the spark that will enable you and your spouse to focus on the important things in life, to learn together, think together, communicate more effectively and express your feelings openly and honestly with each other. Ultimately, a solid, lasting marriage is built by two people in love working it out together.

Every marriage has its ups and downs. But the secret to success is to embrace your problems as opportunities for growth and to press forward *together* for the common goal of a blessed marriage.

Early in our marriage, we faced our differences with disillusionment, disappointment and disgust. "Why can't he put the cap back on the toothpaste tube?" or "Why can't she hang the toilet paper roll the right way?" Little issues soon became big problems, because we did not want to disturb what we thought was supposed to be total bliss by blistering each other with dislikes and disapprovals. However, the attempt to cover up our real issues caused us to sneer and snort at each other rather than simply speak, with compassion, what was on our minds. This attempt to act as if everything was all right got old very fast.

Fortunately, my husband was mature enough to approach me to find out about my apparent "personality change." We both wanted to know what had happened. His initiative opened the communications link of listening and responding—responding and listening, which became an essential key to discovering *who* we were and *where* we were in our relationship. I believe that the greatest barrier between husbands and wives is when they neglect to listen to each other with compassion and forget to talk to each other with love.

Fortunately, we focused on some of the same techniques and strategies discussed by the Goulds in this book, and discovered that success in marriage requires hope, desire, commitment, love, respect and trust. There are no magic formulas for a successful marriage. It takes commitment, supporting each other's dreams and working together to make them a reality. Every couple chooses the quality of their marriage relationship—good or bad.

I've heard it said that marriage is a fifty-fifty proposition. No! No! No! Marriage requires one hundred percent from the husband and one hundred percent from the wife. Unless you freely give all of yourself to your marriage, your relationship will be unbalanced and chaotic. Both spouses are responsible to bring their best to the marriage. It's not always easy, but the rewards are phenomenal.

My husband and I learned to celebrate our differences and acknowledge our weakenesses as well our strengths. We've committed ourselves to help each other work on or deal with our shortcomings.

In marriage, as in life, you can learn by hard knocks or you can get some wise counsel. All of us need help at one time or another. This book offers wise counsel and simple steps for saving your marriage or enhancing the wonderful marriage you have. My husband and I would have been mightily blessed thirty-seven years ago by a book like this. Perhaps we would have made wiser decisions earlier in our relationship. Thank God we finally got it together. There's hope for you!

You have a head start with this book. Even if you already have major differences in your marriage, you can start all over again right where you are. Joe and Debra have done a superb job of teaching the practical, simple truths of staying together through sickness or health, poverty or wealth, for better or worse, until death do us part.

You can make your marriage what you want it to be. It's your choice. Once you and your spouse begin to practice these strategies with each other, you will see the rest of the story begin to unfold. Years from now, you will be able to look back at your marriage and say, "We're living happily ever after."

God bless your marriage.

Thelma L. Wells
Speaker/Author

Introduction

A lot of marriages look good from the outside. To the casual bystander, or sometimes to members of your extended family, the face you show in public is all they see. But as anyone who has been married for any length of time knows, behind the outside appearance is a solid commitment between two people to work together to endure crises, solve problems, cure headaches and heal heartaches.

Of course, marriage is not *all* hard work and determination. Along the way there's plenty of loving, caring, playing, trusting, respecting, nurturing and growing. Sometimes in life the simplest moments can be the most profound. Likewise, in a marriage, a few simple principles can make the difference between falling apart at the seams or staying together for a lifetime of joy, fun and laughter.

This book is about learning to think "together" at three different levels.

The first level is *learning* together. Most people who succeed at marriage become students of their spouse in some way. They study to learn what their spouse wants, needs, likes and dislikes. Both Joe and I went to graduate school, and we discovered that the same steps that helped us earn our degrees also helped us in our marriage. The steps to success are to focus on the subject (in marriage, that means your partner!); then learn as much as you can about the subject; and then apply what you have learned. In school, the final output is a dissertation or a final project; in marriage it's a strong relationship and good commu-nication.

Learning together also means working with your spouse to master the basic skills that are needed in a marriage: among other things how to manage finances, how to make decisions, how to raise kids, how to balance differing sexual drives, and how to resolve conflict. Focus, learn, and apply what you've learned.

The second level of togetherness is learning to *think* together. In other words, not always being ruled by our emotions. Let's say it straight: marriage is an emotional experience. We get dreamy-eyed about our spouse or turned on, and all reason flies out the window. Or tempers flare and feelings get hurt, and all of a sudden we can't talk to each other. Sometimes fear creeps in that our spouse isn't going to love us anymore, or we feel jealous because someone else is working their flirting groove on our husband or wife. At times like these, we need to take a step back and *think* about what is going on, not just react emotionally to the situation. That's hard work. It's much easier to just go with the emotion of the moment, but successful relationships are built on thinking *and* feeling.

The third level is learning to think *together,* which means doing things together, developing common interests, and creating clear boundaries to your relationship that keep others from interfering and messing up your togetherness.

Getting married means sacrificing your personal agenda for the good of the team. Some people simply aren't willing to give up their own racket to be in a committed relationship, but unless *together* is more important to you than *apart,* you'll never survive the tough times that challenge every marriage.

Sacrificing for the good of the team doesn't mean you don't still have your own interests, and it doesn't mean you have to spend twenty-four seven with your spouse, but it does mean that you consider the impact on your marriage of your individual decisions and actions. Ask yourself, "How will what I want to do affect our life together?"

Joe played basketball at the University of Iowa, and if you've ever watched or played basketball, you know there's nothing worse than a ball hog on the floor—someone who is only concerned about getting his own shot. Success in basketball means sometimes giving up your shot to pass to a teammate who has a better angle or better position. Sometimes success means not handling the ball at all but working inside for a rebound. Say what you want about Dennis Rodman, but on the basketball court he (usually) does what is needed to help his team.

Successful basketball teams have five players on the floor, each one maximizing his or her skills, but also blending those skills in with the other players on the team. Marriage is the same way. Both partners need to bring their best individual effort to blend with the strengths and to compensate for the weaknesses of their spouse. Playing like a team is part of staying together.

Another part of learning to think *together* is agreeing that *together* means husband and wife, not husband and wife and all the in-laws, or husband and wife and all our friends. We can learn lessons from how we were raised (good or bad), and we can translate the wisdom (if any) of our parents, our siblings and our friends into our own thinking together, but we must draw clear lines to protect our relationship from outside interference, and always remember that what really counts is what you and your spouse agree upon. When you have kids, you will want to consider their best interests as well, but even then the husband/wife relationship is the most important one.

So there you have it. A simple four-word phrase that covers one of the "secrets" of staying together. Make yourself a sign that you can stick on the refrigerator door: Learning to Think Together.

Learning to think together is for couples who want an enriching and long lasting marriage. Our purpose is to encourage, motivate and inspire you to make your marriage powerful. To be successful requires hope, desire, commitment, love, respect, and trust—there are no magic formulas. In our marriage we haven't done everything perfectly by any means, but we have tried all along to learn from our mistakes, to honor our commitment to each other, and to bring our best to our relationship. That, and a lot of hard work is what it takes to be successful. This book is not a surefire cure or an unconditional guarantee to keep two individuals together. That's *your* job—to work it out together.

Debra and Joe Gould

Chapter 1

Commitment

Commitment is what transforms a promise into reality. It is the words that speak boldly of your intentions. And the actions which speak louder than the words.

It is making the time when there is none. Coming through time after time, year after year.

Commitment is the stuff character is made of: the power to change the face of things. It is the daily triumph of integrity over skepticism.

—Author unknown,
quoted by instructor
at Werner Erhard Forum

Commitments: To love and to cherish until death do us part. To work through the difficult times. To appreciate, respect, trust, and love my spouse forever. To admire the special times, the simple pleasures of being together, to play, laugh, and have fun. To cope with life's challenges. To avoid blame. To embrace my soulmate with all the love I have to give and to seek to understand what makes my partner truly happy. To like my soulmate as much as I love her. *Debra and I believe that our true gift is that we*

1

like each other as friends. Our friendship is the common ground on which we can build. Our love for each other is an added blessing.

Building a strong relationship as husband and wife means not simply *going through* problems but *growing* through your problems together. It's easy to think, and many people do, that having problems means there is trouble in the relationship. While sometimes that's true, problems are also a natural part of living together as two human beings. Rather than muttering to ourselves or complaining to our family and friends about our problems, we need to learn how to embrace our problems as opportunities for growth. Working through problems with your soulmate is what keeps that spark alive, which becomes a flame, which ignites a fire that lights the torch that keeps your marriage alive. Preserving the spark means every day seeking the passion to be together through tough times and happy times. It is giving of ourselves, sharing and crying together through some of the most difficult experiences in life. The joy that we discover in the process of dealing with tough circumstances *together,* is what make our relationships meaningful.

The obvious next question is "How?" How do we keep the spark alive? The answer is simple to say and hard to do. The answer is *commitment.* Commitment is the conscious choice to stay together no matter what. Talk is cheap. Anyone can say, "I love you, baby." And anyone can say, "I do." But commitment means hanging in there even when you don't feel like it. Commitment means doing the right thing even when your buddies say, "Are you going to let your woman tell you what to do?" Commitment says, "Even if you talk me down, I'm going to stay here and work things out, because I love you." Commitment comes out not only through what we say, but also by what we do.

You've probably heard the story about the chicken, the pig, and the bacon and egg breakfast. The chicken who gave the eggs *contributed* to the breakfast, but the pig who gave the bacon was *committed*. Far too often in our relationships, we want to toss in eggs from the sidelines and say, "Here's my contribution." But what is needed if we want the full breakfast, the fully satisfying and fulfilling marriage, is to work our rear ends off to put some bacon on the table. We're not talking about finances, as in "bringing home the bacon," we're talking about committing ourselves to making the marriage (the bacon and egg breakfast of life) complete.

Why do so few couples have a lasting commitment? Often it's because we want part of a relationship (the fun part) without the parts that make the relationship whole. We get out of balance when the part of the relationship we are focusing on is one individual (ourselves) rather than both individuals together. We talk a lot about getting yourself together first, and recognizing what you have as an individual to bring to a relationship, but commitment only happens when you are willing to elevate the needs of the other person above your own needs for the purpose of making the relationship work.

Sometimes what looks like a lack of commitment is actually a lack of courage. Staying committed to someone through thick and thin is not for the faint of heart. At times it can be downright scary. We're not trying to downplay the seriousness of the problems that some couples face. Sometimes your soulmate has personal problems, compulsive habits, or addictive behaviors. Some couples struggle with managing their anger or with chemical dependency on drugs or alcohol. Financial problems are a major source of stress in a lot of marriages. Debra grew up in the projects and experienced poverty first hand. Joe's father moved out when Joe was fourteen, leaving the rest of the family to deal with abandonment and the struggles of a single-parent home. We've been there, and we are very grateful that we are not there today.

Let's call it straight: Life deals out some harsh circumstances. But if you look around, you can find couples who worked through their trials and have a strong, happy marriage to show for it. You can find families who stayed together and learned to deal with hard times, like Debra's family did. What makes the difference?

As a proud African-American man, I desire to be the best husband and father I can be. I desire to wake up each morning and say to Debra, "I love you," and celebrate what we have accomplished together. Out of my desire has grown a commitment never to go to bed angry, and a commitment to look Debra in the eye when we talk and to give her my full attention when she speaks to me. I've discovered that it helps to write your desires down, and then discuss them with your spouse when you're both in a good space in your communication. Timing is everything. If you share your desires when your relationship is rocky, even your purest hope can come across as manipulative, or your spouse might trample on a dream that you hold dear. But in an atmosphere of caring and concern, sharing your desires is a powerful way to show your spouse that you truly care and are committed to the relationship. Sharing your desires with your spouse builds intimacy in your relationship and helps to reinforce your own commitment to the things you say you want.

During the 1996 NBA Eastern Conference playoffs, Dennis Rodman of the Chicago Bulls was interviewed on television. In response to a reporter's question, Rodman said that it takes more than talent to win a championship. A lot of teams have talent, he said, but the teams that also have desire are the ones that rise to the top. Rodman's words really struck home, because I could see a clear connection between achieving success in basketball and achieving success in a marriage. Every couple has the ability, the "talent," to be successful in marriage, but only those couples who also have desire—the desire to make it work, the desire to give unselfishly to each other, the desire to do what it takes to win together—will rise to the top and have world champion marriages. Desire is the fuel that makes commitment work.

Maybe you've never seen someone who modeled commitment. Maybe your father moved out when you were young, maybe your parents never married, but here's some good news: you can choose to be different. You don't have to repeat past mistakes or accept less than the best. You can choose to change and you can achieve your desires.

Often, simply seeing and believing that something is possible is the first step toward making the necessary changes to bring about the desired results. Even though her childhood was often difficult, Debra believed that it was possible to overcome her circumstances. She persevered and graduated from high school, went on to college, and eventually earned her master's degree. In the process, she discovered that success truly is possible.

We're not trying to hold ourselves out as a couple who has all the answers. But we do hope that by sharing our experiences with others we can give you some vision and some hope and show you what is possible.

In *Secret of the Ages*, Robert Collier says that "unless you want something 'the worst way' and manifest that desire in the shape of a strong, impelling force, you will have no will with which to accomplish anything. You must want it as the hungry man wants bread, as the choking man wants air. And if you will but arouse in yourself this fierce, ardent, insatiable desire, you will set in operation one of nature's most potent mental forces."

The key is commitment fueled by desire.

Keys to Save
Your Marriage Every Day

♥ Make a conscious commitment to be together and stay together.

♥ Commit to enriching your marriage by growing spiritually, emotionally, physically, and mentally as an individual, a couple, and a family.

♥ Never go to bed mad.

♥ Commit to working out your relationship together.

♥ Reaffirm your wedding vows every year.

Chapter 2

Images from
Our Parents

Love dies only when growth stops.

—Pearl S. Buck
To My Daughters With Love,
1967

It wasn't until we had been married for five years that Debra realized that we were experiencing the same level of happiness and joy that was evident in her parents' relationship. To this day, Herman and Gloria Washington share and model a commitment to each other that sets an example for everyone they meet. We'll let Debra tell her own story:

Nobody ever has a perfect upbringing, and mine was no exception, but I can honestly say that my parents did the best job they could to establish a solid foundation on which to build a family. Despite the difficulties that go along with living in public housing, my parents stayed together through thick and thin and gave my seven brothers, my sister and me as much love, food, shelter and clothing as they could scrape together. We learned that family is more important than things—although things are nice to have as well.

They protected us as much as they could—although they couldn't be there twenty-four hours a day—but the best thing they ever gave us was a set of values that have stayed with me and guided my life ever since. The most important lessons they taught me as I was growing up were how to be selective about my friends, the power of choices and how to make decisions, and how to preserve my pride and maintain my respect for myself.

Another powerful message that came through loud and clear was "don't dwell on what you don't have; instead, be thankful and show appreciation for your family, your good health, the opportunity to get an education, and that you are blessed with both a mother and a father in the home." They instilled the values of respect, trust, and caring for each other as brothers and sisters, and they taught us to believe in ourselves and to be kind, gentle, and patient with other people. Joe and I can only hope that we can pass along these same values to our son, Joseph.

My parents were typical people who argued and experienced difficulties, just like other folks. But what I remember most are images of happiness not unhappiness in the home. My mother kept the household under control. We took it for granted that things would be in order. She spent time with her children and participated in our Boy Scout and Girl Scout events, even when she had a thousand other chores or challenges in her day. Whatever financial crisis or obligation she was facing, she coped with it. My father worked for the City of New Orleans in maintenance and hustled other odd jobs to take care of his family. He is a proud African-American man who accepted his responsibilities. My grandmother didn't have to raise my parents' children. My father attended every one of his children's graduations, and he walked me down the aisle on my wedding day.

When they were together, my parents laughed, talked, discussed school issues and concerns, and grappled with the difficulties in paying bills. They often made sacrifices to deprive themselves to give first to their kids. Even in their financial struggles they were together. I can still picture them sitting at the kitchen table deciding which bills to pay, whether to rob Peter this month to pay Paul, or vice versa.

My siblings and I were nine children who screamed, fought, and vied for our parents' attention. We competed to see who could be the most persuasive and convincing to talk our parents into buying new shoes for basketball, a glove or bat for baseball, a tennis racket, or a boy scout or girl scout uniform. We had some very creative explanations for why a new piece of equipment was the key to our participation on the team.

I don't know how my parents decided when to say yes and when to say no, knowing that we were surviving on a shoestring budget in the first place. No matter what the outcome was, however, it was fair. Yes, there was disappointment, but never to the point that it caused rivalry or problems in the home. We kids learned the difference between needs and wants. We needed to eat, and to pay the rent and the utilities. A luxury would have been a new pair of shoes or clothing every six months. Instead, it was more like once a year. But through it all we learned to be grateful for food, shelter, and family time. We also learned that there's nothing fair in society and no free rides.

Our greatest form of entertainment was when we gathered on the living room floor to see who could tell the wildest stories or the craziest jokes. These times were full of teasing each other and poking fun. We also used to compare our biggest dreams. Most times we dreamed about more food on the table. We prayed a lot for food and to survive the street gangs.

It never occurred to any of us the added stress we caused our parents. When you're a kid you only concentrate on what's important to you. Somehow, we were raised to appreciate what we had, which was just enough to survive on, and to be grateful for our parents, who were trying to do their best by each one of us. It's not like we had a choice or a vote. It was not our hard-earned money that was being spent, and we weren't the ones working two jobs or more to try to make ends meet. Still, it taught me to appreciate and respect the value of a dollar.

The outside world has its own perspective on the public housing environment. Most people seem to assume that if you live in a public housing project, it's because you have no father, you're ignorant people, criminals, or uneducated derelicts. This biased viewpoint is far from the truth. Yes, we were poor and lived in the projects, but we were not lacking in love, nurture or care from our parents. My mother greeted us when we arrived home from school each day. My father came home every night. My mother prepared a hot meal and we ate dinner together, even if it was pork and beans, or rice and wieners.

Families in public housing want a quality education for their children too. Families in public housing go to church together. They go to PTA meetings and get involved in community outreach programs.

Even today it amazes me how my aunts and uncles and cousins criticize and label public housing. I think it surprises them how well the children of Herman and Gloria Washington turned out. Many of my relatives assumed that, with so many children in one apartment, we would not get along. Because they viewed our public housing conditions in a negative way, they thought we would not complete high school, that we would turn to drugs and end up in prison. Today, some of these same relatives who judged us have children who have brought them pain, shame and despair. Meanwhile, my siblings and I have counted our blessings that our parents instilled in us love, respect, and the ability to get along with each other. Because of the powerful principles that my parents instilled in me, I never once had to ask them to support me once I was grown up.

My parents set such a strong example that it is easy for me to visualize myself in a strong parenting and spousal relationship. Because they were grateful, they taught us kids to be grateful for the simple things we had. Life was hard, but we learned to focus on the positive. I thank the Lord every day that Joe and I have been able to provide a safer environment for our son to grow up in. I'm a witness that hard times can lead to good times if we focus on the positive and work on building character. No one would ever choose hard times, but hard times can make you stronger—if you stay together.

Joe's upbringing was different from mine, and consequently his image of family life and his perspective on relationships was different as well. I'll let him tell his own story:

I was born and raised in New Orleans, where my father worked as a body and fender repairman for the local GM truck dealership, and my mother worked as a seamstress and a domestic. I have two sisters and a brother, as well as two half-sisters from my father's previous marriage, but they didn't live with us. In 1956, when I was five years old, we moved to Ponchartrain Park, the first blue-collar and middle-class suburb for blacks in New Orleans.

Unlike Debra's experience growing up in the Desire housing project, I grew up in a house with a yard, a television set in the living room and two cars in the driveway. Even though my parents never married, they lived together common law and provided a relatively stable and normal home life.

When I look back, though, I realize there were a lot of times my father wasn't around. He did auto body work full time, and then hustled on his off hours painting cars or working overtime. On weekends, he would go out by himself. I remember a time in the fourth grade when my teacher, Mrs. Blanchard, asked the class what our fathers did for a living. When my turn came, I lied and said that my father worked for General Motors in Detroit.

When you're a kid, your idea of "normal" is whatever your own experience is. I thought my family had a perfect life, even though there was conflict between my parents. Today I realize that my father's actions were counterproductive to a good marriage, and my mother's demands that he change didn't help. Their relationship was doomed from the start, I think, because they lived common law instead of getting married. I think my father probably felt he could do whatever he wanted since he wasn't officially married.

You hear some folks say that a marriage license is "just a piece of paper." I disagree. Making a public declaration to be together in marriage, rather than just living together, gives you an anchor *and* a lot of freedom. You can use that freedom—which comes from knowing that your spouse is truly committed to you—to create a successful relationship and friendship that maximizes the qualities and benefits of love. Of course, along with the freedom comes responsibility for making your relationship a work of art that is uniquely yours. What makes a relationship work is freedom and responsibility hand-in-hand with commitment.

Don't get me wrong, I loved both of my parents, and they both worked hard to provide the best they had to offer. I am eternally grateful for what they did to bring me up in this world, but I also realize now the power of commitment, the need to make sacrifices to help a marriage relationship grow, and the importance of establishing common values clearly up front.

As I grew up, basketball became the game of choice and both my brother and I enjoyed some success. In 1964, my brother was a 6'9" regular on the George Washington Carver High School team that won the city championship in our district.

By the time I reached the ninth grade, I was 6'5" and playing on the junior high school team. In 1965, Hurricane Betsy hit New Orleans and flooded our school with more than four feet of water. The gym was ruined and our season was shortened to only five games. After the season, I grew another inch and a half, and when I entered the tenth grade at Carver High School, I began playing for the junior varsity Carver Rams.

About that same time, my father left home. I was fourteen years old and I had never heard him say that he loved me. I know he provided food, shelter, and clothing, but I never heard the words that my heart needed. From that lack in my own upbringing grew a desire and a conviction to say "I love you" to my wife and my son every day. Their love back to me is reassuring and wonderful. If you want further evidence of how this has paid off, my son still hugs and kisses me, even as a young adult.

I learned two important principles from this experience. The first one is a word to fathers: Your wife and your kids need to hear you say "I love you" every day. You may know it's true in your heart, and you may be a good provider of their physical needs, but they need to also hear the words. The second lesson is don't look back and feel sorry for what you missed during your childhood; instead, make a positive difference in the next generation. Just because my father never said "I love you" doesn't mean I can't say it to my son. Maybe your father wasn't around much when you were growing up. You can decide to change that in the next generation by choosing to spend time with your kids. The important thing is to supply for your family's emotional needs as well as their physical needs. You won't do it perfectly, but that's OK. You can rest assured that even if you do your absolute best, your kids will find something to fix in the next generation. I know that my strong desire to tell my son "I love you" is a value instilled in him for life that he will carry into his marriage and into the next generation.

Part of how I coped with my father leaving was by focusing on basketball. During my sophomore season, the team amassed twenty-two victories against only one defeat. I was the starting center and because I was the tallest player on the team, the other students began to notice me. The girls noticed me too, but only to make fun of my height, not because they were interested in me as a potential boyfriend. Anyway, it didn't really matter, because I was kind of shy and basketball was my main passion.

By my junior year, I was 6'7" and our team was a local powerhouse. We had Jimmy Weathersby, one of the city's leading scorers, and we packed the Carver gym with spectators. In the fall of 1967, we were expected to challenge for the state championship. Unfortunately, real life got in the way. Our starting point guard got his girlfriend pregnant and quit school to support his family; another player started hanging out with the wrong crowd and dropped out of school. A couple of other guys were great at practice but could never get it done in the games. Eventually they argued with the coaches and were either suspended or quit.

Those of us who remained on the team had a dismal season, not even qualifying for the district playoffs, let alone state. However, I was fortunate enough to be named to the first team All-City and All-State teams and I was an honorable mention on the High School All-America team. As a result of these honors, I received numerous scholarship offers, including one from the University of Iowa. Freshman coach Lanny Van Eman invited me up to Iowa City to visit the campus.

When I arrived up North, I found one of the most beautiful campuses I have ever seen. I stayed in Iowa for the entire summer and enrolled at the school in the fall. As a young black man from the South, I expected a difficult transition, but it wasn't bad at all. The hardest thing was remembering to enunciate when I spoke, and expressing myself in writing clearly enough for my professors to understand me. The only other thing was getting the proper clothing and equipment for the bone-chilling winters.

My freshman year at Iowa, I was introduced to sex and I developed a slanted view that sexual behavior was something casual. Although I had two long-term relationships while I was in school, I was also sneaking around on the side. I went from being an eighteen-year-old kid with no experience to a twenty-one-year-old man who took advantage of women, although I didn't see it as taking advantage back then.

Out of respect for my wife, I won't elaborate, but suffice it to say I was a knucklehead, bar hopping and trying to pick up women. I knew what I was doing was wrong, but I refused to control myself. The result was broken relationships.

I didn't come to my senses until I was enrolled in a master's program at Southern University in Baton Rouge. At Southern, instead of being a big-shot basketball player, I was just a tall guy going to graduate school. My transition to graduate school was a humbling experience. Instead of the fully furnished one-bedroom apartment and the part-time job I had had at Iowa, now I was living in a dormitory suite with two other guys, I had no money, and I didn't know anybody. And all of a sudden, the young women weren't falling for my lines anymore. I can still remember one woman in particular who seemed to see right through me.

I learned another important lesson. These women weren't looking for a fling with some glamour-talking guy who flattered them; they were interested in building a *future* with a man of integrity and substance. They wanted commitment and respect. My actions came across as childish and immature. They were playing for keeps; I was merely playing.

I knew the consequences of playing for fun when others were playing for real, because I had seen it on the basketball court. In the area where I lived when I was growing up, a bunch of guys my age or a little older regularly played basketball at the park. Most of the guys played at different high schools, which translated into some serious competition. If you came to play for fun and not for real, it was guaranteed you wouldn't be selected to play on one of these teams. Being chosen meant you were known as a serious player who could be depended on to help your team win. I wanted to play, and I practiced on my own to make sure I would always be ready.

It finally clicked for me that women were looking for the same thing from a man. They wanted a guy who was serious enough that they could depend on him, and good enough to help create a winning relationship. Just like in basketball, I needed to work on my own self and polish my relationship skills in order to be ready.

Keys to Save Your Marriage from the Ghosts of the Past

- ♥ If you're playing for keeps, be prepared to bring your best to your relationship.
- ♥ Focus on the positive in your spouse and on building character in yourself.
- ♥ Select your friends carefully. Hang around with people who support your values.
- ♥ If you missed out on something important in your childhood, resolve to make a difference in the next generation.
- ♥ You can choose to make a difference by making different choices. It's never too late to start doing the right thing.
- ♥ Tell your spouse and your children "I love you" every day.

Chapter 3

Don't Compromise
Your Values

Immature love says: "I love you because I need you."
Mature love says: "I need you because I love you."

—Erich Fromm
The Art of Loving, 1956

My first true feeling of independence came when I bought the Red Baron in 1972. The Red Baron was a red, two-door, 1967 Plymouth Belvedere II, with an eight-cylinder 383 engine and plenty of chrome trim. I bought it for $750 from a German student who was going home after graduation. The first thing I did was remove the large U-Haul rearview mirror he had installed on the driver's side. Then I bought an eight-track tape player so I could listen to my music. When I was out driving around in my car, it was as if I was flying above the world, like Snoopy the World War I flying ace in the Peanuts comic strip.

In the summer of 1974, I turned twenty-three, but it was almost like being eighteen again. I was living at home with my mother and I was flat broke. Summer school ended in mid-July, which left me very little time to earn enough money to return to school in the fall. I managed to find a job as a house parent at the K Bar B youth ranch in Lacombe, Louisiana, working 4 p.m. to 8 a.m. with every other weekend off.

One weekend in August, I was off work with no particular place to go. I ran into my cousin Rodney, who was holding two tickets to the Billy Preston and War concert that night at Tad Gormley Stadium. He asked me for a ride to his mother's house, where he was going to call his girlfriend to see if she could go to the concert. If he couldn't reach her, he said, he would call me and we could go together. That was fine with me.

I dropped off Rodney, drove the remaining two blocks to my own mother's house and parked the Red Baron in the driveway. As I walked around the back of my car, a green '67 Plymouth pulled up to the curb, with a very beautiful young woman at the wheel.

That same August day, Debra was on her way to be fitted for her coronation gown for the Southern University homecoming celebration. I'll let her tell her own story:

The university had contracted with a professional tailor to fit our gowns for us. The tailor, Pamela Sherrard, had arranged for the young ladies to meet at her mother's home. I arrived at DeBore Drive looking for this woman's house, but I had forgotten the exact address. I cruised down the street looking for her car, which I was sure I would recognize. I saw a tall man with a charming grin on his face out in front of one of the houses. I leaned out the window and said, "Hey fellow, could you come here for a minute? I'm looking for Pamela Sherrard's house. Do you know her?"

He approached my car, getting his rap on, and said, "She's my sister."

I said, "Yeah? What's your name?"

"Joseph Gould."

Just then, I spotted Pamela's car parked nearby. I said to Joe, "Could you go inside and tell her that Debra Washington from Southern University is here to see her."

By now, Joe was really getting his flirting groove on, and he said, "I'm a graduate student at Southern University in Baton Rouge. I'm home for the weekend. What's your name again?" When I repeated my name he immediately asked me for my phone number.

"I don't give out my phone number to total strangers," I said. "Would you please let Pamela know I'm waiting to see her for our scheduled appointment?"

Joe replied that he was not just any stranger and that he would like to visit with me the following weekend. He was on his way to a concert that night with his cousin, but he insisted that I give him my phone number before he would tell his sister I had arrived for my dress fitting.

For four years during my college experience, I had met several guys on campus who persistently asked for my phone number, but I had always declined. Somehow, Joe was different; there was something unique in his style and appeal. Today, after years of happiness with this man, I know he is a genuine human being with a whole lot of love, passion, and a big heart. But back then, in the brief moment when he was kneeling down to flirt with me, all I knew was that I felt safe. When he flashed his charming, boyish smile, I gave in. I turned off my car and looked inside my purse for a piece of paper to write on. Joe and I exchanged phone numbers that evening, and the rest is history and happily ever after.

Joe and I began courting on the weekends. I was completing my last year of college at Southern University in New Orleans and he was still in graduate school in Baton Rouge. He drove sixty-five miles each way every weekend so we could be together. Of course, we were both living on shoestring budgets so we had to settle for visits at my parents' home, movies, car rides, bowling, parties with friends, and visiting our friends. I think because we started off doing simple and fun things together, we learned how to enjoy each other's company without having to get too fancy or spend a lot of money. The best part was we had a lot of opportunity to talk to each other and to see how the other person treated their friends and relatives.

It was important for Joe to meet my parents and family. My seven protective brothers and my sister wanted to know who this fellow was who had caught their sister's eye. Fortunately for Joe, my brothers all liked him and didn't hassle him. He had a reputation for being a good guy and his basketball success at Carver Senior High and the University of Iowa went over big with my brothers. Joe had been well known in high school and he was respected in the community. He passed the test with my brothers, and my parents liked him immediately.

During the weeks and months that we were dating, we had long conversations about the future. We shared our personal and professional goals. He admired my focus on developing myself and my commitment to finishing my degree. I shared my vision of various business concepts and told him I had an interest in becoming a business owner some day.

Joe understood the importance of what I was accomplishing and how my college degree would support my personal achievements in life. After growing up in the Desire housing project, I was going to be the first in my family to finish college. Completing college was a victory

I had worked long and hard to attain, and my bachelor's degree would be a worthy acheivement.

While we were courting, I never felt pressured by Joe to have sex. He asked me about it a lot, but I wasn't going to compromise my values. There's an old expression, "Why buy the cow when you can get the milk for free?" I understood that Joe was a man with physical needs, but I wasn't going to jeopardize my dreams and risk being distracted from my goals.

He waited, but it wasn't going to bother me if he couldn't. That was not my business. I could only be responsible for my own actions and decisions, and I didn't compromise my values. I made a personal choice and I had no regrets. If anything, our sexual relationship after marriage was better and more satisfying because we were willing to wait.

If I had felt any pressure, most likely I would have told Joe to "keep on stepping, fella." Joe and I are both no-nonsense individuals and he knew I meant what I said. I've never had a problem with asserting myself. My mother always taught me to be true to myself and to take good care of my own psychic satisfaction. I figured that if my relationship with Joe was meant to be, it would happen in due time. I think my excitement, energy, and enthusiasm about life's possibilities truly turned Joe on. I was a focused and charged-up person back then and I still am today. He was ready to share his life with someone who had something to offer him as well, and he was willing to wait for some of the other perks.

Through our years of understanding each other, our bonding and union has been enriched with spiritual awareness, loving, caring, trusting, respecting, and getting through the tough times together. I'm convinced that Joe respected me more because he saw that I respected myself. To this day, I carry myself with pride. My mother used to say, "Always hold your head up high. If a man doesn't want to respect that, then keep on walking, because there's too many other fish in the sea."

I don't understand why women compromise their values. Oh, I see how it happens and I understand the temptation. Joe has always been a sweet talker and, believe me, he played the whole record for me when we were courting. But right up front is the time to let a man know what to expect. Too many women wait until it's too late in the relationship to demand what they want. If you don't give or ask for respect right from the start, it won't happen down the road. You deserve the best. Don't settle for less.

To settle for just any relationship reinforces feelings of low self-esteem. You are a valuable person and as a woman you contribute something unique to a relationship because God created you. If you look at yourself as a whole person, you will discover what you have to offer and then you can ask yourself what you are willing to bring to the relationship rather than looking for someone to give you something for nothing. Learn to love and respect yourself first before you give it away to others. Good men are scarce—and they know it too. But good women also are worth waiting for. Play hard to get, because you want a relationship that meets your standards and value system.

I know some mature women who discovered later in life that if they had concentrated on their values up front, Mr. Right probably would be a part of their lives now. We settle for falling in love too quickly. Our hearts are broken and we become confused about right and wrong. We waste time measuring ourselves against other people's relationships. We say we want what they have in their relationship, but we have no idea the hard work it took for them to get there. Just like the grass is always greener on the other side of the fence, someone else's marriage looks like the ideal.

Joe and I both believe that you make your marriage into what you want it to be. Some people—men *and* women—never slow down long enough to validate their own ideas and their own special qualities or to consider the power of decision—namely that they can control who they want to be and who they want to spend the rest of their life with. Instead, far too many people go through repeated bad experiences, falling in and out of relationships—not love—and never catch on that what they really need to do is learn how to love themselves. Once we learn how to love and respect ourselves, we uncover our inner self and release our inner strength to love other people with no strings attached.

When relationships fail, we're often willing to try again with another partner, but we need to understand that going back to the drawing board really starts with ourselves. We need to respect ourselves enough to look in the mirror, see what needs to be strengthened or changed and then decide what we want and need from our partner and what we are able and willing to bring to the relationship.

A successful marriage starts with you. Establish your values and communicate with your partner up front. Discuss how your values complement each other's to make a stronger relationship. Be good to yourself. It's one thing to compromise on decision making, but never compromise your values.

After we had been dating for six months, Joe proposed. I was not ready for this at all. He told me that he was ready to settle down and I was the woman he wanted to spend the rest of his life with. I was flattered but I could not make this kind of commitment after just six months of dating. I turned him down. The only thing I was willing to commit myself to at that time was finishing my last semester with honors and walking across the stage to receive my hard-earned degree. I wanted no distractions from my goals.

Joe had already completed a successful college career at the University of Iowa, and as an athlete he had done some extensive traveling with the team. He was three years older and had had experiences that I could only imagine or dream about. He had already done what I had only hoped to do. There were so many things I wanted to experience after college myself.

He tried to convince me that we could do all the things I wanted to do—together. I heard him out, but I wasn't going to change my focus when I was so close to achieving my goals. I managed to convince him to postpone the offer. He was disappointed by my response, but he said he understood my position. Nevertheless, he told me that if I turned him down the next time he asked, there would not be a third time.

The next time Joe proposed, he was a little more clever. On the anniversary of our first date, he asked my parents for my hand in marriage. My mother and father sat quietly, then looked at each other and smiled. They were impressed that Joe would consider them enough to ask for their blessing. My father said, "It's OK, if that's what Debra wishes to do."

Later, when Joe and I were alone, he dropped down on one knee and proposed. By this time, I was in my last semester of school and counting the days until my graduation on December 19, 1975. Meanwhile, I had given some serious thought to the idea of working with Joe as husband and wife on our professional and personal goals. I decided I was finally ready. I gave Joe a resounding "yes!" and sealed it with a kiss with tears rolling down my face. When he placed the engagement ring on my finger, I couldn't wait to get to campus on Monday to show my sorority sisters and my co-workers in the accounting department at the Orleans Parish School Board, where I worked part-time.

Later, I asked Joe why he had chosen me from among all the other fish in the sea. He said, "You never compromised your values. You stayed true to your dreams and you had a burning desire to honor your commitments and achieve your goals. I admire your focus, and I love your compassion and your easy way with people." I say this not to brag—although I am proud of what I have accomplished and very proud of my husband—but as an encouragement to others not to compromise their values, to stick to their commitments and to stay focused on their goals. If I can do it, you can do it.

In the years that Joe and I have been married, I've had many women say to me, "Girl, you sure are lucky to have a good man." That's a true statement, Joe is a wonderful man. But it bothers me when other women never seem to give themselves credit for what they bring to their relationships. The way I see it, Joe is just as fortunate to have me as I am to have him. Don't sell yourself short and don't compromise your values. Bring the best you have to offer to your relationship and hold out for a partner who respects you, and you will end up with the partner and the soulmate you deserve.

Keys to Save Your Marriage from the Beginning

♥ Be the kind of person that you would be attracted to.
♥ Don't compromise your values. Anyone who doesn't respect your limits isn't worthy of your time.
♥ Do simple and fun things together. Enjoy each other's company.
♥ Spend time talking—about your feelings, your dreams, your values, your hopes for the future.
♥ Respect your partner—and openly show it.
♥ Thank God for your partner every day.

Chapter 4
Building Bridges

Love is, above all, the gift of oneself.
—Jean Anouilh
Ardèle, 1948

After our year of courtship, I wanted to take another year to plan our wedding. I figured we needed that long to save up enough money to do it right. Joe figured he'd already been waiting long enough and said, "Nonsense. Let's keep it short and simple. The justice of the peace will suit me fine." And just like that, we were embroiled in our first major argument.

I suggested that we involve our parents in the planning and we scheduled a meeting with them. Of course, the first question was, "Have you picked a date?" and once again we were at odds with one another. Joe's mother finally suggested that we concentrate on compiling the invitation list and let our parents, friends and families do the rest.

We set the date for November 8, only three months away, and we kept our wedding plans simple by limiting our wedding party to two of Joe's closest friends, Richard and Terry Gardner, and my best friends Lana Robinson and

Javetta Brogan. My parents arranged for the food, drinks, flowers, invitations, reception hall and entertainment. Joe's mother made the wedding cake, with decorating help from his uncle Louis Gould, who worked in a bakery. Joe's sister, Pamela Grant Sherrard, made all of the formal attire for the wedding party as a wedding gift (it helps to have a tailor in the family), and other friends and family members provided music and photography. We had a few glitches along the way, but by the time our wedding day rolled around, all we had to do was show up for the ceremony. I was the happiest bride in America.

Everything about our ceremony was special, and our reception was complete with lots of good friends, family members, music and food. Of course, on your wedding day the last thing you think about is food, and we left the reception without ever eating. About eleven o'clock that night, we both realized we were hungry. Joe left the apartment for some quick carry-out at Ground Pati's, a local hamburger franchise in New Orleans. To commemorate our wedding night food run, we celebrated our twentieth anniversary with dinner at Ground Pati's.

As everybody knows, saying "I do" is only the first in a long series of commitments and positive statements that provide a solid foundation to a marriage. After the honeymoon glow wears off, it's time to get down to the business of building bridges between two very different people. These bridges, or points of common interest, are the connections that keep a relationship alive and growing. Commitment is the glue that holds the union together and bridges are what keep life interesting and make marriage fun. Joe and I didn't have a concrete plan for building bridges when we were first married, but, looking back, we can see that we naturally did some things that started us off on the right foot.

Getting our own place right away was a step in the right direction. We both enjoyed the peace and quiet with no yelling and screaming from the neighbors, and I was happy to no longer be sharing living space with my siblings.

We only had one car—the Red Baron—so it worked out pretty well when, a few months after I graduated from college, I landed a job as an accountant with the New Orleans District Attorney's office. Joe was already the assistant director for the DA's pre-trial diversionary program for first-time offenders and his division was only two blocks away from mine. We drove to work together every morning and our offices were close enough that we were able to meet for lunch in City Park. The time we were able to spend together commuting and eating lunch kept an open dialogue between us that I think established a healthy pattern of communication in our marriage.

Our mutual faith in God, our regular church attendance, and Bible studies have been three key building blocks in our life together. My family was Baptist and Joe was raised in the Methodist church. After our wedding, I agreed to follow his leadership and attend Bethany United Methodist Church, the same church Joe grew up in and also the church where we were married. Some people might not agree with my decision to switch to my husband's church, but I believe that God set the husband as the spiritual leader in the home, and I chose to honor Joe by going to his usual church. Every couple arrives at their own set of convictions. Whatever your faith is, we both believe it is important for a couple to have compatibility and agreement in this important area. The Bible calls this being "equally yoked." Because your spiritual perspective guides and determines your decisions and your approach to everyday life, you're only asking for trouble if you and your partner don't agree on what you believe.

We attended the 8:00 a.m. service every Sunday, and after church we stopped at Joe's mother's house for breakfast. She had supported the family when Joe was growing up by working as a domestic, cooking for rich white families in New Orleans. She could sure put on a nice breakfast and it seemed to give her a real charge to have us stop by each week. Part of our Sunday ritual included playing tennis at a community playground in the Ponchartrain Park neighborhood. It gave us more time to talk.

Sunday was also the day to visit with my parents, and they loved to see their daughter and son-in-law. Joe could do no wrong in my parent's eyes. He loved to joke with my dad and tease my mother. My mother was like a little girl when Joe was around. If he didn't find something to tease her about within about two minutes of walking in the door, she blamed me.

"What's wrong with Joe? she'd say. "He's not laughing today. Are you feeding your husband? Are you taking care of your womanly duties? I know you, Debra, you are so spoiled. Did you make Joe angry?"

I would just laugh, because she was fishing for a problem if her son-in-law didn't come right in to see her and give her a big hug and a kiss and tease her a little bit. I always said, "No, Mother, there is nothing wrong in our marriage. Just stop a minute and listen to the men yelling about the football or basketball game on the television. I hate to tell you, Mother, but you play second fiddle to sports. Don't worry, Joe will make his grand entrance soon enough."

Joe had spoiled my mother just the same way he spoiled me—with his attention and affection. It was contagious. And when he did finally enter the kitchen to greet my mother, she would smile as though he had just parted the Red Sea.

During the week, we made time after work for some type of recreation. With our first income tax return as a married couple, we bought two bicycles and a bike rack. We rode for fun and for exercise and once again we had plenty of opportunity to talk. Recreation played an important role in establishing strong roots for our relationship. Whether side by side on bicycles or across the net on the tennis court, we had many opportunities to get to know each other in different environments. Find something active that you and your spouse can do together. Whether it's riding bikes, playing golf, or working out at the gym, staying physically fit and in good health contributes to an energized and productive life and a fun and exciting relationship.

Weekends were the time when we were really able to stretch out and enjoy ourselves as a couple. We went to several dances with friends who were members of social clubs. We also enjoyed a local night club called Lou and Charlie's, where we could catch live jazz acts on the weekends. One of Joe's former classmates performed with one of the bands, and we enjoyed listening to him play.

We also enjoyed nights out at the theater, watching plays like *Mahalia,* with Jennifer Holiday, and Shelley Garrett's *Beauty Shop*. I preferred musicals and Joe liked comedies, but the most important thing for both of us was being together. We started attending the theater while we were dating, back when Joe was trying to impress me. After a while, I became used to being wined and dined and going to exciting new plays. Growing up in the projects, I had never been exposed to the theater, and Joe took great pleasure in introducing me to some of the finer things in life. After the show we would sit and talk over coffee, and I fell even more deeply in love with my wonderful man.

During our first few years together, we were fortunate to be invited to dinner parties with other couples who also were enjoying their marriages. Talking to husbands and wives who were committed to staying together and making their marriages succeed was a great inspiration to us. The seeds of this book were probably planted during those early days when we experienced first hand the value of surrounding our marriage with good role models who were willing to share honestly about their struggles and what they were doing to make their marriages work. Many of these friendships have grown and flourish-ed during the past twenty-three years, and we are grateful for all of the couples who have shown us the way over the years.

Another outlet for Joe was playing basketball in amateur and commercial athletic leagues. Most of the players on the team were married, so the games provided family fun. Joe used to worry that I would be bored by his passion for basketball, but I always enjoyed watching him do something that he loved and that he was really good at. And even if I did get bored from time to time, that's part of marriage too. Sometimes you just go along because you know that your spouse is having a good time. Goodness knows that Joe has gone along with me many times when he didn't necessarily want to. He would say that he puts up with a lot from me.

A case in point is the time we took a six-week disco dancing class together. Joe knows that I like to dance, and

I always thought he did too. He would pick me up after work and we would eat a light dinner at a nearby restaurant before our hour-long class. It wasn't until years later that I heard him confess to a friend in a joking manner, "Debra gets me enrolled in some of the goofiest things—like disco dancing." But to his credit, before I could pounce on him he added, "But that's my baby and if she's having fun and it brings a charming smile to her face, then that's all right with me."

To draw a principle out of our experience that would apply in any marriage, I would say learn how to keep your antenna up for what pleases your spouse, and then be willing to make a change—or even a sacrifice—to make your partner happy. If you learn how to give unselfishly to your spouse, I guarantee you will receive more than your fair share in return. And in the process you might even learn to love something that you had never before considered— like disco dancing.

Not everything went smoothly, of course, during our first few months together. I'll never forget the first time I tried to cook for Joe. I was already intimidated, because his mother was a gourmet cook who had worked as a domestic in some wealthy homes. When I was a girl, dinner was already ready when I arrived home from school. I never gave cooking much thought and I never learned any of the basic skills. I spent most of my time in sports or other activities.

The first few weeks, I spent every day on the phone with my mother-in-law. She would calm me down and talk me through my meal preparation. I wanted to cook something that Joe would like, so I tried his mother's recipe for smothered steak in gravy, with brown rice and a steamed vegetable on the side.

Before I got my hands on it, the steak was a beautiful piece of meat. Joe's mother told me how to make the roux for the gravy, but I made it too thick. When Joe came home, everything smelled good in the kitchen, and he eagerly removed the lid on the skillet to check things out. When he used a big fork to pick up the steak, everything in the pan came up with it. The roux had hardened like clay. He started laughing and said, "What's this?"

"That's the steak you like," I said.

He laughed some more and said, "I'm not eating this. No way."

I started crying and said, "I'm never going to cook again!"

"Hey, baby, let's go to McDonald's." Joe likes to tease a lot, but the more he laughed the madder I became. Finally I threatened to walk out and go back to my parents. Joe just laughed some more. He told me, "Debra, you're taking this cooking stuff way too seriously. Just relax, it will come to you sooner or later." Still, he refused to eat the steak.

My mother-in-law must have really loved me, because during my first year of marriage she coached or helped me prepare most of our dinner meals. For the first seven years, I cooked strictly from a cookbook or her recipes. I never deviated from the step by step instructions. If I was missing an ingredient, I would turn everything off and go to the grocery store for that item.

Joe was fascinated watching me cook. He always said that I took everything too seriously, but I think he also understood and appreciated that I was trying to please him by getting cooking down to a science. And, yes, it seemed he was always laughing at me. I often wanted to strangle him but, as bad as it was at times, I never killed him with my cooking.

Keys to Save Your Marriage for Yourselves

♥ Develop common interests and enjoy your time together.
♥ Expand your horizons. Learn to love the things your partner loves.
♥ Cultivate a common faith. The couple that prays together stays together.
♥ Give your partner room to grow.
♥ Exercise together and stay physically fit to energize your relationship.
♥ Surround your marriage with good role models and couples who will keep you honest.
♥ Agree to preserve peace and harmony in your home.
♥ Keep faith and hope alive.
♥ Don't give up on cooking. Learn together if you both don't know how.

Chapter 5

Setting Boundaries

To love is to choose.

—Joseph Priest
Meditations of a Parish Priest,
1886

Building bridges establishes a strong relationship between married partners; setting boundaries protects the marriage from undue outside influence. One of the biggest challenges a couple faces in marriage, especially in the early days, is making a clean break from the families they grew up in. Debra and I believe what it says in Genesis chapter two, verse twenty-four, that a man is supposed to leave his father and mother and stick to his wife, and the two of them become one flesh. The point is, when a couple gets married they establish their own separate little family, just the two of them, and their relationship with each other becomes primary.

When our son finds his soulmate and moves to establish his own household, Debra and I will honor his need to leave us in order to become one flesh with his wife and establish their own family. Our commitment is not to interfere in his marriage relationship and to allow him to

39

live by his own standards. By that time, we trust we will have trained him well, and we pray that he finds a genuine and caring woman who will love him as much as Debra loves me (and vice versa), and someone who will stand by him through thick and thin.

The three main sources of conflict for most young couples and their families are time, money, and the grandkids. One of the first issues that a newlywed couple has to decide is how much time they will spend with the relatives, versus time spent alone or with friends. Usually, holidays are the first major battleground, because you can only be one place at a time, but if you live in the same town with both sets of in-laws, every weekend could be up for grabs. It's important to decide early on how holiday decisions will be made, and how much other time you will spend with your extended family. There's no right or wrong answer, but it's important that both husband and wife agree on how these issues will be settled.

Money, both borrowing and lending, can be a very touchy subject with the in-laws. Every couple should reach an agreement on how to handle financial matters within the family. Most problems arise when there is not a clear understanding of the terms of a loan. Because the transaction is taking place with a member of the family, it might seem like it would be showing a lack of trust to put everything in writing. But if agreements are not written down, you run the risk that the other person's memory of what was agreed upon will differ from your memory or expectations. Debra and I both experienced situations where we didn't get paid back when we loaned money within the family. I think some people saw us making certain purchases and figured we were living large and wouldn't miss the money if it wasn't paid back. What they didn't see was all the blood, sweat, and tears that Debra put into juggling our budget to save some of our income each month so we could buy the things we want. Someone who borrows money doesn't see the impact of that loan on our ability to meet our own debts and monthly obligations. I finally put my foot down and established a policy that Debra and I would not loan money to family or friends.

Of course, if you do make a "no loans" policy, or whatever you decide, both partners need to stick to the agreement. Debra never has any problem with this. She's the type of person who has no trouble making and keeping exact commitments, and she expects the people around her to hold to the same standard. I tend to be more laid back, which has gotten me in hot water from time to time. Debra will tell her family point blank, "No, I can't loan you any money," or "I need to talk to Joe about that." I, on the other hand, have gone against the policy a few times. Debra gets mad because I was the one to suggest the rules in the first place, and then I don't always live by them. She tells me I'm trying to be a big shot with my family, but I think I'm just trying to help people out. The important issue in a marriage is that both partners agree to whatever policies the two of you decide on, and then you should respect your spouse enough not to go around the rules on your own.

Grandchildren also create opportunities for conflict within a family. Issues of proper discipline or disagreements about how often the grandparents should be able to see their precious grandkids can lead to a lot of stress. One area in particular where my family wanted to weigh in with their opinions was on the timing of our starting a family. When Debra and I had been married five years, we were still having fun just the two of us. My mother was convinced there was something wrong with me—that I couldn't father a child. She wondered whether I had been made sterile when I had the measles or mumps as a boy. And she was vocal with her opinions and questions.

At the time, I could have gone either way, but Debra wasn't ready yet to be a mother. She had grown up in a family with a lot of people housed in a small area, and she was comfortable for the time being with just the two of us. She was still enjoying coming home to peace and harmony and a quiet evening alone with her husband. We always had fun and exciting things to do nights and weekends when we wanted to. We both believed it was important to get to know each other well before we started a family, and we wanted to be free to do some of the things we had talked about when we were dating.

My mother would have none of it, and she didn't let up. She wanted grandchildren. At first I just ignored her comments, but then she went to work on Debra.

"Don't wait until you are too old. By now you should have had at least two or three children."

Debra politely objected and made a request to talk about something else.

My mother said. "I'm just looking around and seeing all the other young ladies your age with two or three children. It's time for you and Joe to settle down and start your family."

It was obvious that we were getting nowhere with my mother. Debra wouldn't even allow herself to get mad after a while because she knew my mother meant well and that nothing we said was going to change her viewpoint. Debra respected her and didn't want all of their conversations to escalate into arguments, so she simply said that when we were ready we would have a baby. I gently told my mother that she would be the first to know, and in the meantime she should stop interfering with young folks' decisions. Of course, my mother never did quiet down until Debra announced that she was pregnant.

The main point to glean from this story is the importance of setting definite boundaries around your marriage relationship, to be firm but polite with your family. We still love the families we grew up in, but we have established clear boundaries with our parents, siblings and cousins to keep them from crowding our relationship and having unreal expectations of us.

It's like in sports. If nobody chalked the lines on a baseball diamond or a football field, the players wouldn't know what was out of bounds and what wasn't. Once the lines are clearly drawn, however, everyone can see where to concentrate their activities. Our extended family is welcome to cheer us on from the sidelines, but they don't belong on our playing field. It doesn't mean they won't try to rush onto the field like an excited fan from time to time, but at least when that happens everyone will be able to see that they are out of order.

Like any two people trying to build a marriage, Debra and I have experienced some uncomfortable moments with our families. At times, both my mother and my sister have taken it upon themselves to challenge my family role as a brother, son, and husband, as if I'm supposed to choose between them and Debra and Joseph. I keep it really simple. I tell Debra, "You are my wife. You come first. What is there to decide or choose?"

I don't waste my energy on the mind games that my family plays. They say things like, "My brother Joe will do such and such when we say so." I tell Debra that my commitment is to her, and she and Joseph are the ones who I come home to every night. I see the games that my family plays and I tell Debra that if she wants to entertain their games it's up to her, but for me it isn't worth it.

I'm not saying we should never spend time with our extended family or never listen to what they have to say, but I am saying it is important to set my first priority on the needs and concerns of my own family unit and to make my own decisions with my wife. Debra and I figure we have gotten pretty good at knowing what works in our household without opinions from everybody else. Our simple rule is that we don't argue with our in-laws, and we keep our decisions in-house.

Your family may try to test whether blood is thicker than water. If you want your marriage to grow and last, you need to communicate clearly to both your spouse and your extended family that your marriage commitment is thicker and stronger than blood. Debra and I decided long ago to keep family out of our business and household affairs.

Like any couple, we have our share of disagreements and problems that we need to work out, but we figured out early on that the only two individuals who can get to the root cause of our problems and solve them are Joe and Debra. Not only have we agreed to keep our family decisions in-house but we also keep our disputes just between the two of us. Debra's brothers and sister will tell her parents about issues going on in their homes, but we have observed that sometimes after the two individuals have worked out their differences, others on the outside still harbor grudges or have hard feelings toward one person or the other. The problem is that they are given information about the situation but they are not a part of the conflict resolution so they have nowhere to go with their feelings after the problem is over. Debra and I have learned to handle our marital problems ourselves and to keep our parents and siblings out of it. Debra tells me that she doesn't want to tamper with the respect that her parents have for me by airing out our differences on the family clothesline. In the end, our parents cannot manage our marriage for us. We want them to see that they raised responsible individuals who can work out their difficulties as adults. Every couple has a certain amount of trouble. Any time you put two different personalities behind two sets of opinions, you are bound to bump heads at some point. But we have chosen to address our issues up front. Debra deserves to hear any problems directly from me, and vice versa. Instead of feeding the gossip mill, we choose happiness over confusion, trust over distrust, and honor over lack of respect. Debra and I have chosen to stay together and to resolve our differences together.

Fortunately, Debra and I have never felt the need to separate, but Debra always tells me that if she ever did need to get away for awhile she would check in to a hotel to think things through rather than running home to her parents. Parents are usually in favor of their children whether they are right or wrong, and Debra has said that she doesn't want her parents siding with her if she is wrong or harboring resentment against me if I am wrong.

Part of the consequences of keeping our stuff in-house is that our families assume that we never have any problems because we're not shouting them from the rooftop. Of course, when people think you have the perfect life, they expect you to act perfectly all the time. If Debra or I ever do raise our voices, it seems like someone is always there to say, "I thought you guys never argued." Or if we're not together in public, like at one of Joseph's high school games, all I hear is, "Where's Debra? I thought you two were never apart." At times like these, Debra and I just laugh. We take it as a compliment that other people see something in our marriage that they admire, but we know that we are far from perfect.

Several of our extended family like to live out of comparisons. They like to tell Debra and me that we have things easy. From our perspective, problems and challenges are just something that every couple goes through. There's nothing easy about it at all. Our lives are imperfect because we are imperfect people. What makes the difference is how you choose to deal with your problems—do you dwell on the problem or focus on solutions? We cannot control what others think, feel, believe or say, but we know between ourselves that we have had to work out our share of disputes and differences.

It is important to build a boundary against negative thinking, whether it comes from inside your marriage or from family, friends, or acquaintances. Some people don't know how to succeed other than by trying to tear others down to build themselves up. Negative people are like crabs in a barrel—always trying to climb up on someone else's back and then pinching everyone around them. Some people just seem geared to give you all the reasons why something won't work, without ever once considering the possibility that success is achievable. Even if you realize that their negative behavior is rooted in their own unhappiness or sour life circumstances, after a while it wears you down. But as difficult as it is to be gracious toward someone else's weaknesses, we all want others to be gracious toward ours.

Debra and I get along well because we communicate with each other, we're straightforward with each other, and we don't have any hidden agendas. We enjoy each other's company and we allow each other space to breathe. On top of that, we have learned how to establish boundaries that allow us to work out our relationship together without pressure and interference from people on the outside looking in.

Keys to Save Your Marriage from the In-Laws

- ♥ Leave and cleave. Make a clean break from your family of origin.
- ♥ Guard your time alone as a couple.
- ♥ Establish firm boundaries and each partner take responsibility to communicate clearly with your own family.
- ♥ Don't run to your family or friends in times of trouble. Stay home and work it out.
- ♥ Don't live out of comparison. Establish your own standards and live by them.
- ♥ Don't allow family or friends to run in and out of your home unannounced.
- ♥ Neither a borrower nor a lender be.
- ♥ Always speak highly of your spouse in front of family and friends.

Chapter 6

Raising Kids Together

The love we give away is the only love we keep.

—Elbert Hubbard
The Notebook, 1927

Deliver us, Lord, from the excessive demands of business and social commitments that limit our time for family relationships. Relieve us from insensitivity to our children and the harshness of judgment that prevent understanding. Save us from domineering attitudes and the selfish imposition of our will, and guard us from softness and indulgence that we mistake for love. Bless us with wise and understanding hearts, that we may demand neither too much nor too little, and grant us such a measure of love that we may nurture our children to the fullness of manhood or womanhood which thou hast purposed for them. Amen.

After a routine semi-annual checkup when I was twenty-six years old, my gynecologist asked to meet with Joe and me to discuss some concerns about my health. She told us that I showed signs of serious endometriosis and that she was uncertain whether I would ever be able to bear children. After we had waited for five years since our marriage to start our family, this news was devastating. The doctor suggested that I stop taking my birth control pills for three months to give my body a rest. When I returned to the doctor to determine whether I should resume the contraceptives, she discovered it was already too late. Of course, Joe was quick to take credit and he couldn't wait to gloat to his mother, who had suggested he was sterile.

In February 1980, I was planning to attend the Mardi Gras Zulu Ball with my sister-in-law Pamela. I met her at my mother-in-law's house, and I was wearing the gown she had made for me when I was homecoming junior maid back in college. When Pamela saw me, she said, "That gown is fitting a little tight, Debra." She thought she was teasing me until I answered her remark. "It's tight for a good reason, Pamela—I'm pregnant."

"Hallelujah," Pamela shouted. "Hey Mom! Did you hear what Debra said? She's pregnant!"

The two of them made such a fuss over me that I began to wonder what they were on. They hugged me and kissed me and my mother-in-law started calling all her friends.

"Sit down, get off your feet," they said. "Can we get you anything?" I was thinking that some room to breathe would be nice at that moment. After I had given them all the details about how far along I was and when the baby was due, we finally left for the Zulu Ball.

"Don't keep Debra out too late," my mother-in-law

admonished Pamela. "And no drinking, Debra, do you hear me, girl?" At the time I didn't drink alcohol anyway, so she didn't have to worry.

The rest of that week, my mother-in-law called me every day, and when Joe and I went to church on Sunday, everybody was touching and feeling my stomach. You'd have thought I was the first woman ever to be in such a condition.

The birth of our son brought us so much joy. After five years together, Joe and I agreed we were ready for this next exciting phase of our lives, but there's really no way to anticipate how a newborn will alter your relationship. When that little bundle is handed to you for the first time, it changes your perspective on life forever.

If we had a son, Joe wanted to name him Jay Gould, like the millionaire, or possibly Justin. He didn't want to name him Joseph, because he was trying to break up the sequential series of names. We agreed on the name Jessica if it was a girl. Either way was fine for me, because the initials J.G. had already brought so much joy and happiness into my life.

The day our son was born was a warm and sunny Saturday afternoon. Joe was outside hitting a tennis ball against the wall for practice and I was mopping the floors. I didn't have any labor pains, but I did have a strange sensation in my stomach every ten minutes or so. I had been to the doctor the day before and she had said that I was getting close, but that no one could tell exactly when I would go into labor.

Around 1:30 on that Saturday afternoon, I just had a sense that I should go to the hospital. My mother had said that a woman will always know when it's time. I called Joe inside and told him how I was feeling. We were both really calm at this point. We had been planning to attend my friend Renette Dejoie's wedding later that afternoon and Renette had jokingly told me that my baby could come on any day but November 8. Oh well. Joe and I gathered my overnight bag and left for the twenty mile drive to Lakeside Hospital.

When we arrived, an attendant brought me a wheelchair while Joe parked the car. By the time he arrived inside the hospital, Joe was getting anxious because I was still filling out paperwork. Finally, I was wheeled to my room and my doctor and the anesthesiologist were notified. By this time I had begun to experience some mild pain, and when the anesthesiologist arrived he gave me an epidural. Joe and I settled in to wait. To pass the time we watched *It's A Mad, Mad, Mad, Mad World* on television. While we were laughing our fool heads off, the young lady in the next room was screaming loudly. When I heard that she had been in labor for close to twenty-four hours, I was nervous, because I figured it was only a matter of time before I was yelping myself.

After a while, the nurse came by to examine me again. Suddenly, she turned to Joe and said, "Well, father, are you ready to go scrub?" She called an orderly into the room and said, "Let's move Mrs. Gould into the delivery room now, and summon Dr. Gilotra quickly." The nurse told me I was dilated to seven centimeters and I was almost ready to begin delivery.

I remember being extremely cold in the delivery room, but otherwise I felt great. When Dr. Gilotra arrived, she asked me a few questions and began to prepare for delivery. It seemed like only a matter of minutes before I heard the doctor asking for a pair of forceps. I panicked when I saw the shiny metal tongs and quickly asked what was happening. Dr. Gilotra told me that everything was fine, but that the baby needed a little encouragement to come into this world. Joe kissed me and said, "Relax. Dr. Gilotra is a professional."

The next thing I knew, the doctor was congratulating us.

"It's a boy!"

Joe kissed me on my forehead and I cried. The nurse wrapped our tiny son in a blanket and Dr. Gilotra brought him over to me. As this new little person was placed on my chest, I felt warmth for the first time in the chilly delivery room. If you have ever been in the delivery room as a mother or a father, you know how that wonderful moment feels.

When it was Joe's turn to hold his son, he held him up and said, "Let's name him Joseph Gould III." When I said, "OK," Joe looked at little Joseph and said, "Son, you will know every day of your life that I love you, and I will care for you forever."

When the nurse came to take Joseph, Joe gripped my hand tightly and said, "I love you, Debra." I looked back at Joe and told him that today was the second best day of my life, "after the day I married you, Mr. Gould."

The next morning, Joe arrived at the hospital with flowers and a small gift package with some jewelry inside. He said, "I wanted to give you something special to say how much I love you and to thank you for being the mother of our son."

Joseph Gould III opened up a whole new world for us. All of my attention shifted to parenting. I didn't want him out of my sight. Before we had even considered starting our family, Joe had told me that he would want me to stay home from work for one year to care for our baby.

At the time, I was more into developing my career and I didn't give his words much thought. Now it was time to face that decision for real. Joe said he realized it would be a big sacrifice for me to put my career on hold for a year, but it was important to him. He didn't have to twist my arm, because I was really getting into motherhood. Joseph arrived at a perfect time in my life. I felt transformed by this beautiful new human being and I didn't want to be separated from him. Still, I told Joe that if I was going to take the time off, when I returned to work I wanted a housekeeper, Friday nights out for dinner and dancing, occasional weekend excursions with my husband, and a regular family vacation once Joseph was old enough. Joe agreed to my terms and I made the transition to full-time mom for a year.

Joe could not wait to get home in the evening to play with our new son. He loved saying the word *son*. While I prepared dinner, Joe would bathe the baby or sing songs, read and play with him. I had decided to breast feed Joseph for at least six months, but after that Joe became very particular about what the baby would eat. He hinted that he wanted me to prepare fresh fruits and vegetables for our son rather than feeding him commercial baby food. He told me to read every label before I put anything in Joseph's mouth. Like a nut I did it. Joe wanted only cloth diapers for our baby, so we had a diaper service. I was agreeable to everything, because, like Joe, I wanted the best for our son.

Before I knew it, a full year had flown by and we were struggling with the reality of trying to live on a single salary. I didn't want to put our son in child care, but we needed the extra income and it was time to go back to work. I could barely comprehend how someone else could care for my child. It was a difficult decision to make the transition back into the workplace, but Joe assured me that everything would be all right. We arranged with a retired couple in the neighborhood—the parents of one of Joe's buddies—Mr. and Mrs. Saizon to care for our son. They loved Joseph and cared for him for three months until the wife became ill. We now had to find a new baby sitter.

We asked Joe's mother for assistance and she took a short leave from work to care for Joseph while we looked for a new caretaker. Eventually, some close friends of hers, the Andersons, volunteered to help us. For the next year and a half, until Joseph was three, Papa and Grandma Anderson completely spoiled our son. Two things he never lacked were attention and love. Eventually, however, he Joseph became too active for the Andersons to care for him, and we started our search for a pre-school or day care center.

When Joseph started nursery school, we began to meet other couples with children. We began to socialize with other families, especially those whose kids were playing sports at the park. The faces changed from time to time as Joseph progressed through school, but being around other families that were staying together reinforced our own commitment to provide a stable home for our son.

Both Joe and I understood that parenting was a big commitment and responsibility. We had agreed long before Joseph came along that we would raise our kids together and not become a burden on our own parents. They had spent their best years caring for us when we were growing up and we wanted them to enjoy their grandchildren without being saddled with them. Our family rule was that our kids would visit their grandparents only with us, that we would not drop off our children for our parents to care for them. We wanted to establish a positive family structure in our home, instilling our own values in our kids. Aunts and uncles, cousins and grandparents would serve as extended family. We believe that any couple that isn't prepared to take on the full responsibility of parenting should wait until they are ready. To this day, I believe our parents appreciated that Joe and I were committed to parenting and took responsibility for raising our son.

My health problems persisted even after I had my baby. When Joseph was two years old, Joe and I talked about having more children. We continued to have an active sex life without contraception, but I never became pregnant. I don't recall ever being frustrated about not getting pregnant, and Joe said he was satisfied with the way things were. He was the happiest man in the world, he said, because Joseph and I made his life complete. He wanted to relieve my mind and let me know that the most important thing was that I knew he loved me totally. I thanked God for giving us Joseph, and every day I cherish the precious gift he is to us.

I began to experience other complications, such as fibroid tumors, and I had two surgeries over the next ten years for this condition. I gradually adjusted my mind-set to enjoying our family of three. I often think about how I might have missed the gift of Joseph, but God was gracious, and I am thankful that my husband was happy and contented with his only son.

As it turned out, having just one child worked well with our active lifestyle, but I have always tried to be careful not to be an overactive or smothering parent. My parents allowed me to soar like an eagle, and I want to extend the same privilege and spirit of freedom to my son.

Joe has always taken an active and vocal role in raising Joseph. He tells our son every day that he is a blessing in our lives and that he is a one-in-a-million miracle. "Long before we knew you as Joseph," Joe says, "you survived and fought your way through conception and the birthing process. There were millions of other sperm swimming around that never connected with your mother's egg. You won the battle, and now the rest of your life should be a piece of cake. You came here with a fighting spirit, and you were already special long before we knew you personally. Take this story as an anchor and remember as you live in this world that you are great, not because your mother and I tell you that you're great, but because you now know how powerful you have always been. You are a warrior. Discover your own greatness in this life and be the best Joseph you can be."

The highlight of my day is the pure joy of watching father and son interacting. The bonding, nurturing and friendship between my two Joe is incredible. I wish the same for every father and every child. Both Joe and I encourage every man who reads this book to invest his time, energy and attention in his sons and daughters. It's the best gift you can give your children and yourself.

As his mother, I have often told Joseph that we are here to shape his will not to break his spirit. We have promised to mold him, love him, help him and care for him. His job is to dream big dreams. Joe and I desire to be actively involved together in every aspect of Joseph's upbringing, whether it's planning, academics, athletics, or extracurricular activities. We have made a strong commitment to keep our family spiritually enriched through regular church attendance and Bible study. Through simple acts of kindness to each other, we empower ourselves to live life to the fullest. Motherhood has certainly elevated my perspective to want to create a safe home environment, to be a well-respected person who is dependable, to love my family and to be of service to others.

I thank my son for helping me to grow as a mother and as a person. I have had the wonderful experience of loving, caring, trusting and giving to others that I almost missed by chasing my career path. Thank you, Joseph, for slowing me down long enough to look into your eyes, to hear your laughter, and to see your energy for life. Every parent has the choice to embrace all of these wonderful experiences and emotions—but it takes commitment and it takes an act of the will. The payoff, however, is priceless.

The first year of Joseph's life, I nursed him and cuddled him, and I didn't want to associate with the outside world. But as he grew older, there were more outside activities and interests to explore. From age three to six we enrolled Joseph in a Montessori program. Most of our new couple friends we met at the school. Most families took turns hosting weekend activities. It was like borrowing each other's kids for playtime and it gave the parents a chance to get to know each other.

Our days of attending only the worship service at church were now over. Joe and I began attending an adult Sunday School class so that Joseph could participate in the children's Sunday School. We wanted him to spend time getting to know the kids at church and relating to Bible teachings at his level. Joe always wanted to be the one to pick up our son after the class was over.

Because we attend the same church where Joe grew up, the elders used to tell me stories about when Joe was a little boy. As I watched my husband take on the father's role with his own son, it was like seeing history and the future come together in one place. Our time on Sunday was a magnificent snapshot of strong African-American men at church, reminiscing about their upbringing and checking out the new generation. As I witnessed my son begin to feel a sense of belonging, I was glad I had agreed to worship at Joe's church. When it comes to worshipping the Lord and being active churchgoers, I believe it is healthy for a family when the father takes the lead.

The importance to your children of having their father in the home cannot be overstated. Of course we all recognize that the mother is indispensable, but the absence of a father's daily presence in the home leaves a void in the lives of children that cannot be filled. Joe's father moved out when Joe was fourteen and, although Joe is grateful for the years when his father was around, he felt an immediate impact when his father left. We have also seen the fallout from dads who bail out in our extended family and in the community at large.

Before we were married, Joe used to spend a lot of time with his nephew, whose father was off dealing with his own circumstances. Once I came along, and then Joseph, Joe's attention appropriately turned to his own immediate family and he didn't have as much time available for his nephew. Joe later found out that his nephew really missed the times they had spent together, and the two of them had a chance to talk things through. Their discussion revealed that Joe's nephew was jealous because our son Joseph was the only cousin who had a father in the home who took an interest in him and went places with him. The nephew said to Joe, "Joseph has a home, he has his own room, he has a mom and dad, he travels on trips with you and Debra—he goes places with you all the time. Uncle Joe, you used to take me places before he came along. Your family reminds me of the Cosby family on TV. You're happy all the time and you go to church together too." Having a father at home doesn't turn a family into the Cosbys, but in a nutshell, Joe's nephew summed up what walks out the door when fathers leave: stability and continuity, a sense of wholeness and connection, and the child's confidence that he or she is worthy of the father's attention. For generations, mothers have done their best to fill the void, and many have done a mighty job of preserving their families, but a mother shouldn't have to play two roles, and the result just isn't the same as having Dad at home. Men, I understand the circumstances that cause many of you to leave (or never be there in the first place), but the best gift you can give your children—and give yourself, for that matter—is the gift of a stable home. Like so many other things in life, it boils down to commitment.

I learned an important lesson during my upbringing through observations that my mom wanted to run the show all the time. My dad would let her have her way. When my brothers would disobey my dad's orders to take care of chores, or to come straight home from school, or to come inside before it was dark, my mother would intercede on my brothers' behalf and argue with my dad in front of my brothers. It caused confusion in the household and I'm sure that my father viewed it as form of disrespect.

In my own marriage, Joe doesn't play that game. When our teenage son tries to enroll me in discussions on his point of view after his dad has asked him to do something, my position on the matter is simple. I tell Joseph that "your father is the man of the house, and when he asks you to do something, that's it."

"Well, Mom—"

When Joseph tries to rationalize his behavior, I reply, "Thank you for sharing your perspective, but you still have to accept responsibility for what your father has asked of you." I allow him to express his thoughts and viewpoints, but if his father has told him to do a task or stick to a curfew, then that's what must be done. Trust me, it is hard to stay neutral, but from my own childhood I learned the importance of both parents presenting a united front to the kids. And unless you are a mind reader and know exactly how your spouse would respond in every situation, the two of you had better talk things out—in other words, communicate. I was a child who tried to play my parents against each other just like my brothers, and I didn't like the outcome. It made my parents upset and created tension in the house. In the end, whatever racket I was trying to sell was not worth the unhappiness.

One of the hardest things to maintain in a marriage once the kids arrive is time alone with your spouse. I think I had women's intuition or something when I told Joe I would only stay home for Joseph's first year if Joe promised that we would have Friday nights and occasional weekends alone together. A wonderful marriage is built on the foundation of a good relationship, and the only way to preserve that good relationship is with time. I not only love Joe as my husband, but he's my best friend, too, and I want to spend time with my friend.

Joe gets my full attention when we are together and our son knows that Mom and Dad are going to spend some quality uninterrupted time together for the first few minutes after we arrive home from work. Those first ten to fifteen minutes are our precious time, our opportunity to reconnect, to get back on the same page and to make sure we are communicating.

One rule we have consistently agreed upon is never to go to bed mad. We've stayed up pretty late on occasion, but we have always settled our misunderstandings and worked out solutions to our disagreements. Joseph hasn't been privy to *everything* over the years, but I believe he has learned far more by watching the give and take in Joe's and my relationship than by anything we have ever said to him. Achieving happiness and peace in a marriage takes hard work and dedication, and our children learn by our example.

Keys to Save Your Marriage When the Kids Come

- ♥ Stay together. The best gift you can give your kids is a stable home life.
- ♥ Don't argue in front of the kids.
- ♥ Back each other up. Don't let your kids divide and conquer.
- ♥ Don't neglect your spouse after the kids arrive. Make time to be alone together.
- ♥ Discuss and agree on the changes in your time schedules, sexual intimacy, and finances.
- ♥ Deliberately teach your children your values, morals and beliefs.
- ♥ Raise your own kids. Let your parents be grandparents.
- ♥ Build your children's sense of worth by loving them unconditionally.
- ♥ Tell your kids how special they are and instill in them a vision for greatness.

Chapter 7

Juggling Finances

The sum which two married people owe to one another defies calculation.
   It is an infinite debt, which can only be discharged through all eternity.

—Goethe
Elective Affinities, 1809

When Joe was a kid, his parents would sometimes argue about his mother's spending. It wasn't that she was a foolhardy spender, but she wasn't always disciplined with the pocketbook. Joe picked up a lot of his mother's spending habits. In his own words, "I buy what I need first and I buy what I want second, which usually means there's nothing left over for savings." For me, not having some money set aside each month for savings is simply not acceptable. Like a lot of couples, we were set up for conflict when it came to money.

Because arguments over money are one of the leading causes of marriages falling apart, it is important to estab-lish right from the start how financial decisions are going to be made. Ideally, these discussions will begin even before you get engaged or married, so that you can start your marriage out on the right foot monetarily. Even if neither partner is a strong financial manager, help is available from CPAs, financial planners, and investment managers.

In most relationships, one partner is a better money manager than the other. I majored in accounting, so in our house I have always been the one to handle the finances. I saw to it that we established a family budget and financial goals as soon as we were married. Every six months, we sit down and review our professional and personal goals to make sure we're still on track. Joe has acknowledged that my ability to plan and my disciplined spending habits have been good for our family and our relationship, but it hasn't always been easy. Joe and I agreed on a joint checking account to handle expenses and emergencies, but our savings account was established in my name, because we both knew Joe's spending habits.

Joe turned his paycheck over to me each time and I managed our budget. We maintained monthly limits on credit card spending, but Joe would often exceed his limit. When that happened, he would ask me for part of my portion, because I rarely spent my allotment. He always told me that I was too tight and hard on myself and that I should learn to let go and live a little more dangerously. He told me to relax and leave my accounting job at the office, but I always responded by reminding him of the goals we had set, one of which was to save twenty percent of our annual income. Our savings account was initially divided up into retirement savings, an education fund, savings to purchase a house, and a contingency amount for emergencies. Joe supports all of these goals and in his mind he understands that saving money is important, but sticking to the budget to make sure we have enough set aside for savings has always been a challenge for him. I have always been one to save money for a rainy day. I have no problem with being disciplined, but Joe's procrastination and spending habits have led to abusive expenses and living above our means from time to time over the years. I always tell him that it takes a strong woman to keep things going. He says, "I guess I can't argue with that."

I also like to plan my shopping excursions. When we have a choice, we usually buy better quality items, even if they cost a little more, because we know they will last longer and be a better investment over the long term.

My first ride on an airplane was to go with Joe to a law enforcement conference in Washington D.C. While we were there we had an opportunity to visit Joe's father, who was living there at the time. On this trip, I caught the travel bug, and planning for our annual summer vacation became a part of our budget. Every year now, a portion of our savings goes into our vacation goal account. I figure out where we can afford to travel and still maintain our budget. Joe still struggles with keeping his spending under control, but, thanks to my focus and discipline, we still get to travel and enjoy ourselves.

We lived in an apartment for three years, until we thought we had enough in our savings to begin looking for a house. When we started looking at properties, it seemed everything we liked required a larger down payment than what we had. When Joe's parents offered to help us, we were grateful for the assistance. His father sent some money to bolster our savings and we were able to afford a townhouse in a subdivision called Parc Brittany in East New Orleans. We moved into our new home in December 1978. We continued to use Joe's old college furniture, because we both still had college loans to repay and we wanted to maintain our other goal accounts. I always said,

"Let's take it one step at a time. Let's get into the house and get used to paying a mortgage before we add a bunch of other expenses."

One of the ways that I saw to conserve money and stay on our budget was not to spend money on going out for lunch every day. To me a sack lunch was just fine. Joe hated this idea with a passion. All his co-workers at the district attorney's office went out for lunch and Joe was embarrassed to walk into the office every morning carrying his brown paper bag. My focus was on saving and getting ahead, but Joe wasn't buying my logic. He said he wasn't going to argue about it, but he also wasn't going to carry his lunch to work. I knew I would only frustrate myself by continuing to push my point about budgeting, so instead I made adjustments in our vacation goal account and we cut back on our weekend entertainment to free up enough cash for lunch money. We started entertaining more at home, inviting close friends over to watch television or play cards or other table games. Most young couples probably face similar decisions when they are starting out, but it seems as though making adjustments and compromising is also an ongoing part of financial management in a marriage.

Financial pressure can come when one partner decides to quit a job in order to pursue something else, or when a wife changes careers to become a stay-at-home mom. Sometimes you don't have a choice in the matter. Joe had worked for the district attorney's office for ten years when he was laid off in 1985. He was able to take his retirement pay to pay off credit card debt and to fix some problems we had with our car at that time, but then he needed to find another job to replace the income he had lost.

He was able immediately to move into a lesser job as a resource instructor for an adult education program.

The pay wasn't what we were used to him bringing home, but it was a great experience for Joe and very inspirational because he saw people who were looking for something out of life and who were willing to pursue their dreams. The job was humbling financially, but rewarding spiritually. Not only that, it was fun for him.

Joe also took a part-time job in outside sales for a water treatment equipment company. Selling door to door was an education in itself. Much like an athlete, as a sales rep you practice all your plays before the big game, and then it's just you and your potential customer going one-on-one out on the front porch. And just like in a marriage, perseverance and persuasion pay off in the long run.

As Joe began to enjoy some success in his new endeavors, he realized that what he really wanted to do was start and run his own business. He attended several chamber of commerce meetings and started the networking process. He wrote down the pros and cons of working for someone else versus starting his own business. He conducted a few surveys and researched possible career opportunities. Finally he decided to pursue his own business.

He had always been good at sales, because he has a wonderful attitude and is such a people person, but he still wasn't sure what would be the best use of his skills. I didn't know what to say to motivate him, but I trusted his judgment and believed in him enough to know that he would make a good decision.

Out of his retirement money from the D.A.'s office, we set aside a six-month cushion to take the immediate financial pressure off his mind and to free up his creativity. I dipped into my personal savings to get us through the difficult months that followed. I wrote to our creditors and adjusted our monthly payments. I cooked every night to avoid unnecessary dining out and I paid our bills on time to maintain a good credit report. I still had my health plan at work so our medical needs were covered.

Along the way, Joe met a man named Joe Cummings, who had a successful advertising specialties company. Mr. Cummings was willing to teach Joe the ropes and soon my husband was back to his natural self again, walking like a powerful eagle as the head of Joe Gould Advertising Specialties, Inc. Business has fluctuated over the past ten years, but Joe's company is holding its own in the marketplace.

Managing finances and staying on a budget require day-to-day, ongoing discipline. Problems can begin to occur when you start to make more money than you are accustomed to having and your budget begins to expand as a result. Parkinson's Law says that "work expands to fill the time available to do it," and finances often work the same way. Budgets expand to use up all the dollars available—and often more than what's available. If you don't keep your eye on the bottom line, gradual and subtle changes take place until one day you wake up and realize that you are generating more overhead than income and your finances are out of control.

During the heyday of Joe's advertising specialties business, and with my continued income, we moved into a larger home and took on more financial obligations. With the new house, we added expenses for decorating, furnishings, and yard and pool maintenance, in addition to a mortgage that was twice the size of our previous payment.

After we had been living the good life for some time, we were hit by a downturn in Joe's business, partly due to his habit of putting things off, but also in part because of a reduction in business from some longstanding customers. To compensate, Joe has had to actively sell and market his business more than before. We also were forced to sit down and review our budget to clear up our high debt ratio. A return to some of the conservative habits we had back when we first married and a lot of perseverance have put us back in better shape financially. We want to encourage you that no matter how messed up your finances may be, you can always make changes. Start wherever you are and take the next step you can to restore financial sanity to your home.

It happened to us and I've seen it happen to others, that in the name of success, achievement and performance we drastically complicated our lives. In the process, through the steps we have taken to dig ourselves out of our predicaments, Joe and I have grown and matured, and we have learned some important lessons about keeping our life simple.

Keys to Save Your Marriage Financially

♥ Set realistic financial goals that you both can work to accomplish.

♥ Establish a budget that includes savings and charitable giving.

♥ Stick to your budget. Don't live above your means.

♥ Budget for dates and weekends away, especially after you have kids.

♥ Let the stronger money manager set the plan, but manage your finances together.

♥ Get outside help from a financial planner or CPA before you get in over your heads.

Chapter 8

Supporting
Each Other's Dreams

Love is that condition in which the happiness of
another person is essential to your own.

—Robert Heinlein
Stranger in a Strange Land,
1961

When I was younger, I focused my energy on advancing my career in the district attorney's office. I never gave much thought to owning my own business. Many people work at the same job or in the same field for years and never consider what they might prefer to do. When I was laid off by the DA in 1985, I was a husband and a father with a small boy, and Debra and I had our share of financial obligations. Although I had been given advance notice of the layoff, I still had no idea what to do next when my last day on the job arrived.

When I lost what had seemed to be a secure position, it was a blow to my ego and my self-confidence. Debra did her best to encourage me, but my self-image was bouncing all over the place. Probably the most important thing that Debra did for me during that time of great uncertainty was to assure me that, whatever I chose to do next, she was behind me one hundred percent. Debra believed in me, even on those days when I didn't believe in myself.

The positive side of being let go from your job is that suddenly the whole world of possibilities opens up in front of you. It took some time and quite a lot of effort, but as Debra explained in the previous chapter, when I finally met Joe Cummings I began to develop a vision for starting my own advertising specialties company.

Meanwhile, Debra had always harbored thoughts of operating her own public speaking and consulting business. Because she was motivated, disciplined and focused, she set about making her dream a reality. She knew that she would need more work experience, training and skills to achieve her goals, because an African-American woman who wants to step out had better have her act together. This is still the good ol' USA, and folks won't give you the time of day unless you have your credentials and can prove what you can do. Debra decided that graduate school was the next logical step.

Even before I lost my job with the district attorney's office, she was talking to me about registering for classes. We had to set her plans aside for a time while I worked through my own transition, but after she supported me through my business start-up, it was time for me to also support her dreams. To succeed in marriage, it's important for both spouses to understand and rally around the other's hopes and dreams, whatever they may be. And the only way to know your partner's desires is to talk them through. I will admit that Debra is much better than I am at sharing her dreams, but I have learned over the years how to listen, when to speak, and how to be encouraging.

Debra worked out a plan to continue her full responsibilities for parenting, cooking, full-time employment, and homework. She scheduled her classes in an extension program from Florida Institute of Technology on nights when I could be home with Joseph. She cooked and froze meals on the weekends and labeled what I had to heat in the microwave. We had a housekeeper who kept the place tidy throughout the week, but it seemed like Debra was doing laundry almost every night.

I took over some of the household duties, such as running errands and grocery shopping, and I even cooked occasionally when Debra was too burned out. I also attended PTA meetings and went with Joseph on his Boy Scout outings, school field trips, camping trips and sports activities. During this time, he and I truly cemented our bond as father and son, because we were spending so much time together. I could tell that Debra sometimes wanted to slam her books shut and come wrestle with us or go on an outing with us, but she stuck to her routine.

Graduate school was a two-year commitment, which Debra took on in the middle of an already busy schedule, but if there's one thing that sets Debra apart, it's her ability to finish what she starts. She made do with four or five hours of sleep per night, and she studied in the morning, at lunch and every night after Joseph and I were in bed. Her weekends were spent at the local university library for peace and quiet. I always told her that keeping her calendar full and running non-stop was what kept her batteries charged, but even with her high energy, the pace of life took its toll. Nevertheless, through perseverance and determination, she earned her master's degree in management.

After Debra received her graduate degree, she continued her job in project management with Boeing Petroleum

Services, but she was raring to go with a business venture of her own. At that time, my business was going through its ups and downs and it didn't seem like a good idea to have both of us self-employed. Debra's heart said to pursue her aspirations in professional speaking and consulting, but logic dictated that she keep her daytime job.

With her typical drive and passion, she looked at every aspect of making her business dreams a reality. We talked it over time and again, but we always came back to our financial obligations and our lifestyle. Even after we modified our living expenses and determined what we could live without, we were still uncertain about the wisdom of venturing out. I could tell she was frustrated when we agreed to put her plans on the back burner for the time being.

In the meantime, she sought the counsel of friends in her network and she joined a professional association to learn as much about the available opportunities as she could. Don't worry about what you can't do; take the step you can. One of the steps that she discovered she could take was giving dinner presentations for her professional group. Before long, she had expanded into weekend workshops, teaching time management, goal setting, and team building. As she began to expand her list of contacts and referrals, it started to appear more viable to venture out on her own.

One day Debra started talking to me about trying to become entrepreneurs together. Up to that point we had talked about being vice presidents in each other's business, but we had not seriously considered the prospect of working together. Debra's vision was for me to also develop my skills to become a professional speaker. With my experience making sales presentations, she thought I was a natural who could deliver motivational and inspirational messages to larger audiences.

The interesting thing to me about Debra's idea was that I had had similar visions long before I met her—except I had imagined myself speaking in the political arena. I had enjoyed some college classes on municipal government and politics, and at one time I had entertained notions of pursuing a career in public service. Often when you are on a path, you don't arrive at the same time as someone else, but you arrive at the same place. As Debra and I continued to discuss our options, we began to develop different scenarios for how to make it work.

On my way home from work one day, I stopped to visit my mother. She reminded me about a time when she and my father were still together and my mother had talked about starting a business. In 1965, hurricane Betsy hit the city of New Orleans and flooded an area below the canal called the lower ninth ward. Her vision was to buy a piece of property below the canal, because people were moving out and they were selling their properties cheap. My mother wanted to find a parcel where she could have a bakery shop for herself and an auto repair garage for my father, who did auto body and fender repairs. According to my mother, my father was not interested in the idea, and they separated not long after.

After my father moved out, my mother quit her job and started her own lunch plate business, selling hot meals like barbecued ribs and collard greens, and macaroni and cheese out of the back seat of her '55 Chevy. I would often ride along with her to keep the food from sliding all over the car between stops. She worked out a route that covered construction sites and other outdoor workplaces, and those workers had the good fortune of being treated to my mother's great down home cooking. I didn't understand at the time how much courage and faith it took for her to go into business for herself, but she was a strong and talented woman.

I learned from my mother's experience the importance in a marriage of supporting each other's dreams and working together to make them a reality. Some people act as though something "out there" is stopping them from having what they truly want in life. I'm here to tell you there is nothing holding you back except yourself.

Part of Debra's and my vision is to leave a legacy for our son—a legacy of economic empowerment and the inspiration to make his generation even better than ours. Debra's grandmother had only a third-grade education and most of her family were sharecroppers, but they had a vision for making things better for the next generation. Debra's mother finished high school and her father finished three years of college before joining the U.S. Navy, and they had a vision for making things better for the next generation. Both Debra and I completed college and went on for advanced degrees, which opened up opportunities for us that our ancestors could only dream about. We want to take the advantages that we have earned (and that our parents and grandparents prepared us for) to make things even better in Joseph's generation. We are pushing him in school to always give his best and we have gradually exposed him to my business to prepare him for the possibility of taking it over someday if he chooses. With his ideas and creative thinking, he may be able to take the business to another level. Our legacy is to prepare the next generation to build on what we have built, not simply to sit back and enjoy the fruits of our labor.

Debra and I haven't yet achieved everything we

want to accomplish, but by working together, we have made significant progress toward our goals. In addition to my advertising specialties business, I am the executive director for a non-profit agency for senior citizens. Debra does professional speaking, training and consulting through her own business, Debra Gould & Associates, LLC.

The point is not to focus on the specific things that Debra and I are doing, but to encourage you and your spouse to consider your own interests, your own hopes and dreams, and to take action to make them a reality.

Keys to Save Your Marriage from Stagnation

- ♥ Expand your horizons through reading and listening to motivational tapes.
- ♥ Encourage each other to grow spiritually, emotionally, professionally and personally.
- ♥ Support each other's dreams, take on new challenges and build your future together.
- ♥ Don't withhold problems from each other. Grow through the difficulties together.
- ♥ Learn how to plan and how to follow your plan to achieve your goals.
- ♥ If you're a goal setter, don't overwhelm your spouse with a complete life map. Start out with a few, achievable goals that you can agree on.
- ♥ Succeed together and then raise your sights.
- ♥ Leave your children a legacy of economic empowerment and the inspiration to make things even better in their generation.

Chapter 9

Fear and Atmosphere

There are six requisites in every happy marriage.
The first is Faith and the remaining five are Confidence.

—Elbert Hubbard
The Notebook, 1927

If you honestly try to support your partner's dreams, sooner or later you will bring to the surface your hidden fears about your own success, achievement and performance. Most men want to generate enough income to support a comfortable lifestyle, with a nice house, a car they can be proud of, and clothes that make them look good. The fear that most men harbor inside is not being able to provide adequately for their families, or getting swallowed up in the process.

When I was young, an occasional bully would appear in the neighborhood. We would try to avoid him, but sometimes that just wasn't possible. My friends and I used to say that the only thing between us and the bully was fear and atmosphere. Any man can walk through atmosphere but not many men can walk through fear.

In the neighborhood, the bully could be armed and dangerous, and a little bit of fear was probably not a bad thing, but when it comes to achieving what you want in life, you need to look in the mirror. You might be surprised to discover that the bully is you. Now what do you have to be afraid of? If you conquer your fear, then the only thing standing between you and what you want is atmosphere— and anybody can walk through that.

One way to overcome fear is to face it together with your spouse. I know that many men like to picture themselves as rugged individualists, and the last thing we want to talk about is what we are afraid of, but let's face it, we all need encouragement and emotional boosting along the way. When I was in transition from my job at the district attorney's office to what I am doing today, I had to make my own decisions about the exact job that I thought I could do well and enjoy, but Debra gave me a fresh perspective and her consistent encouragement helped me to keep my focus on becoming the best I could be and not settling for second best. Fear may be a hurdle, but if you see yourself as a sleek track star, then hurdles are no problem, they just keep the race interesting.

As we head into the twenty-first century, the traditional roles in many relationships have changed. As a result, many men feel pressure or fear mentally, socially, physically and economically. As societal norms have changed, many men have begun to live out of comparison. Rather than holding to a standard based on how they were raised or what they believe, they begin to look around and make evaluations about how they measure up against the guy next door or the man down the street. If a man feels as though he measures up, then he feels good, but he feels guilty when he perceives that he is falling short.

The problem with living out of comparison is that you hand responsibility to somebody else for how your life is turning out. There will always be someone who seems to have it better than you, and whenever they are around, you will feel inferior. But if you hang out with folks who seem to have it worse, you might feel better for a while, but eventually you lose your vision for how much better life can be. Part of building good boundaries around yourself and your relationships, which we discussed earlier, is to decide what *you* believe and how *you* want to make decisions, and then live accordingly.

Many men respond to their mental fears by withdrawing socially. I know when I was looking for work, the last thing I wanted was for someone to ask me "how's it going?" When a man (or a woman) is living out of comparison, he ends up with self-imposed feelings of inadequacy, which tend to drive him into his shell. The best thing we can do as partners in a relationship is to offer encouragement to our spouse to build his or her self-confidence.

The traditional role for a man in a marriage is to be the protector, defender and provider for his family. Many of these ideas have been written off lately as "obsolete cultural norms," but the truth is men are naturally wired to gain satisfaction from protecting and providing. When a man gives up this role, or has it taken away, he tends to become passive.

Back when physical strength was more important on the job, men could easily fulfill these roles, but as the workplace has changed, the opportunity for men to protect and provide has also changed. It hasn't gone away, but its nature has been altered. The good news is, we can choose to be proud men who protect our families from negative outside influences and who provide stability and encouragement in our homes.

Most men are not comfortable when their spouse generates more income than they do. Some men will say they don't mind, but in our society, a man who appears to be economically dependent is viewed as a wimp—if he chooses to live by comparison.

In our ever changing society, the fear for women might be, "Can I do everything I want to do without sacrificing the things that are really important?" Though much has changed, there still is an undercurrent that women should be willing to settle for less. Debra and I have always had a traditional home where she looks to me for leadership, but that has never meant that she shouldn't be developing all of her skills, interests and abilities and finding productive ways to express her gifts. Just as any man submits himself to authority but still gives his best when he goes to work, a woman doesn't become "something less" when she submits to her husband's leadership in the home. A lot of women today seem to struggle with this idea, but in the couples we know where the different roles of husband and wife are understood and respected, both partners flourish in the relationship. Over the years, we have had to make some tough decisions about work, education and child care—the same kinds of decisions that many couples make—but by working together we have found ways to meet our family's needs and to allow Debra to pursue interests outside the home that have truly ful-filled her abilities. The best thing we can do for our wives as husbands is to encourage them to blossom in all their gifts.

No perfect set of guidelines exist for creating a relationship between two human beings, but the people we know who have long lasting relationships with each other tend to have a similar purpose and vision, which is anchored in their declaration to be with each other. Where there is no vision, the relationship will perish.

Of course, any time you put a man and a woman together, misunderstandings and lack of communication cannot be far behind. In our marriage, Debra and I are rarely on the same page about money. She likes to save every spare nickel and I like to buy what I want when I want it. She also wants to establish family, spiritual, professional and personal goals, and then stick to them. My approach has always been more laid back.

Early in our marriage, I could eloquently tell Debra all the wonderful things I wanted to achieve in three months, six months, one year, five years or ten years, but she wanted to write everything down and then develop a step by step plan for how to accomplish what we said. She would say, "Before we deviate we should openly discuss whether the goals are unrealistic, insignificant or need restructuring; but whatever the case, we should talk it out. Doing nothing is not an option."

I have always been one to procrastinate. If I came up with some goals but then didn't start to work on them right away, she would accuse me of not keeping my word or say that I lacked integrity. She said, "I would rather have you not say anything than to make something up and then assume it's a done deal. I hear you out there boosting and bragging with your family and your buddies, but I see no evidence that you have performed any of these things."

We struggled with this concept for more than a year before I truly understood her ideas and expectations. Even then, I didn't really like her point of view. Part of the problem was that it seemed she was always bringing stuff up while I was watching sports on my day off. If I tried to suggest that we talk at another time, she would see it as one more procrastination.

For a long time, the situation did not improve. She was always riding me and I was ignoring her viewpoint. One day Debra was listening to a motivational tape about building healthy relationships. The speaker said that sometimes a couple needs a facilitator to help them work through their differences. Debra looked in the Yellow Pages and made a few calls. She made an appointment with a family counselor and went by herself for a few weeks before asking me to join her. My first response was that I didn't want to be spreading our problems around, but Debra pointed out that a neutral counselor was better than confiding in our family. Like a lot of people, I thought counseling was only for people with major problems, but I have since come to understand that counseling is good even if your problem is simply a lack of effective communication. Debra and I both think that more couples should go for counseling earlier in their relationships, before small problems grow out of control. Even the healthiest marriage has issues that a counselor can help to resolve—and we say the sooner the better.

I finally agreed to go, out of respect for Debra, but I didn't think we would accomplish anything and I had a lot of anxiety and reservations. During our fifth and sixth sessions, the counselor began to draw some critical attitudes out of me that Debra had never heard before. She said, "Now I'm sorry I put both of us through this. On the other hand, if we are going to grow as a couple, we need to be upfront and honest with each other." The counselor suggested that I come in alone for the next few weeks without Debra so that he and I could discuss some of the issues that had come up.

During those one-on-one sessions, the counselor helped me to face some of my own attitudes that were getting in the way of my relationship with Debra. He showed me how Debra was pushing some buttons from the past that I was unwilling to deal with. I realized that I had been trying to fake my way through my marriage, but Debra was challenging me to step up and live out my goals. She expected me to bring something to the table besides talk. Her aggressiveness was intimidating at times, but I realized that she was expecting the best from me because she loved me. I realized that I needed to get my act together or risk losing my beautiful soulmate. For the first time, I really understood what was important to Debra and what I had to do to make our marriage grow. In short, I was in for a lot of hard work.

When I came home from each session, Debra would probe me to find out how everything was going, but I didn't want to analyze my progress until we were both back with the counselor. I said, "It's killing you not to know, isn't it?"

At our next joint session with the counselor, he helped me to articulate what I had learned. I told Debra that I wanted our marriage to be based on truth and strength in knowing that we genuinely love, respect and care for each other. I knew that she possessed some complementary qualities that would make me a better man if I would listen to her. I needed to show my integrity by making my words mean something when I said them. I needed to do a better job of communicating how I would achieve the goals that I committed to on paper. And I needed to be honest about my feelings. I told Debra that it would never be as easy for me to open up as it was for her, but that I would do my best. Debra learned that she needed to help me by listening more and talking less. I told her that I would stop making excuses and that I would reevaluate my goals.

We continued our counseling sessions for several more months, and the reuniting we experienced was deep and powerful. Our relationship truly moved to a higher level. At the early stages there was a lot of fear and we were very uncertain about the outcome. But in the end, it was a blessing. Debra said she was rejoicing because her man loved her enough to give counseling a try. I'm grateful that Debra took the giant step to get us started. I would say we were a happily married couple with a few stepping stones to cross, but counseling definitely showed us the way across the river. Don't wait until your relationship is drowning. Find a facilitator who can help you and your precious spouse learn how to communicate more effectively. Remember, the only thing standing between you and the marriage relationship you would like to have is fear and atmosphere.

Keys to Save Your Marriage from Fear

- ♥ Take responsibility for your own life. Don't blame other people or circumstances for what you are afraid to confront.
- ♥ Be honest with your partner.
- ♥ Agree on roles that work for both of you.
- ♥ Don't worry about the Joneses.
- ♥ Confront your fears together. Learn to embrace uncertainty and move forward anyway.
- ♥ Stay positive and encourage your spouse.
- ♥ Go for counseling before you need it. Even the healthiest relationships can use help with communication and problem solving.
- ♥ Make your home a safe haven physically and emotionally.

Chapter 10

The Little Things

There is no more lovely, friendly and charming relationship, communion or company than a good marriage.

—Martin Luther
Table Talk, 1569

Sometimes when there is conflict in a marriage, it seems like the hurdles are insurmountable. But the steps required to make a difference are often short and simple. What makes a peaceful home is simply loving, caring, nurturing, supporting, trusting and downright being good to each other. I don't mean to minimize any serious problems that you are facing in your marriage, but just make sure you aren't making things too complicated. Do the little things that make a big difference.

Joe remembers going in to the body shop with his father when he was young. His father taught him how to sand out the body of a car to prepare it for painting. Joe Sr. always said to slow down and take a uniform approach to work. Sand back and forth a little section at a time, not in big swirls where you might miss something. The result was a smooth fender that was ready for painting. What the customer saw on the outside—a flawless coat of paint— was the result of painstaking attention to preparing the underlying metal through a series of small steps.

This lesson applies to relationships as well as to auto bodies. In a marriage, taking a uniform approach, carefully handling the little things that might never be seen on the outside, instead of swirling all over the place and missing what's important, prepares your relationship for the finishing touches—the colorful splash of paint— that everybody sees. The final product from the body shop is a fully restored automobile. The product of "the little things" in a marriage is a happy and fulfilled spouse and a fully restored relationship.

Early in our marriage, Joe developed the habit of leaving me little notes around the house to brighten my day. He would say something like:

> Debra,
>   Thank you for all your special qualities
> that you bring to my life.
>   My spirit is often touched by your com-
> mitment to life. I admire your quest to live
> life to the fullest and I consider it a special
> privilege to walk this path with you.
>   Love always,
>   Joe

The exact words are not important; what counts is that he writes from his heart. If you are just getting started with doing the little things, don't concentrate on how embarrassed you might feel to say something tender to your spouse, but focus on the warmth and joy that your words will bring.

No matter how hectic our business days are, Joe and I take the time to check in just to say hello to each other. If I'm not available, Joe will leave a short but sweet voice mail message designed to lift my spirits. Often he will recite a cute rhyme or a poem, or some other bit of inspiration to brighten my day. When we were working on this book, I surprised Joe with a tape recording of all the voice mail messages he had left me, which I had saved.

When we get home at night, before we open the mail or start the evening meal, we look into each other's eyes and say, "How are you doing?" We hold hands and kiss and listen to each other's challenges and stressful events of the day. Sometimes I even cry to release my pain and hurt, but we manage to get through it all because we are there for each other. It's important during this time to truly listen to what your spouse is saying. Don't allow yourself to be distracted by your own agenda.

Sound corny? Well, don't knock it until you've tried it. I've discovered that a lot of people like to criticize things they have never tried, but this simple routine has done a lot to keep Joe and me connected in our marriage. I know of individuals who say they want to be alone when they first get home, but then they never get around to connecting as a couple.

After Joe and I have had ten or fifteen minutes to unwind *together*, we proceed to restore our lives with what's left in the day, and we avoid dwelling on the difficulties that everyone faces daily. Sometimes we have to keep busy to chase away the negative stuff, by starting the evening meal, washing clothes, putting out the trash, cutting the grass, gardening, or reviewing homework.

During supper we have family time, which is uninterrupted quality time with no phone calls. It's amazing how many families never sit down for a meal together. We give thanks for our many blessings and talk some more about the events in our day. As often as possible, we have thirty minutes for family reading following the dinner hour. We usually eat our dessert during this time. Sometimes Joe or Joseph will share the corny joke or riddle for the day, and then there's nothing like a challenging game of Monopoly or Scrabble. What we choose to do during this time is not as important as simply being together. The highlight for me is the laughter and joy we bring to each other. The problems are still there, but Home Sweet Home is our safe environment and we just leave our burdens on the doormat.

Building a marriage relationship is an every day process. Each new day, you are entitled to make your life look like you want it to look. This precious jewel is often handled carelessly, but every morning you receive the gift of another twenty-four hours. Spend it wisely.

Fifteen Little Things
to Save Your Marriage

♥ Say "I love you" every day.
♥ Leave love notes and voice mail messages.
♥ Call your spouse every day just to check in.
♥ Discover the little things your partner likes, and do them often.
♥ Show appreciation and praise your spouse often.
♥ Forgive and forget. Start each day fresh.
♥ Keep your sex life exciting.
♥ Look for the positive. You'll find it.

♥ Don't criticize and don't get mad about little things.
♥ Remember to celebrate important days and events.
♥ Take time daily for each other.
♥ Listen.
♥ Don't lie.
♥ Learn to laugh.
♥ Let your spouse win.

Chapter 11

Ya'll Still Married?

There is nothing nobler or more admirable than when two people who see eye to eye keep house as man and wife, confounding their enemies and delighting their friends.

—Homer
Odyssey

When Joe and I go out dancing or to a concert, it amazes me how many people will say to us, "Y'all still married? Most folks by now have been married two or three times. What's your secret?" If the person asking is a guy, I usually prefer not to respond, because somewhere along the way Joe and I have probably encountered that individual tiptoeing in the night without his spouse.

One friend in particular saw Joe and me playing golf, playing tennis, dancing in a club, and bike riding. Finally he stopped to ask us what kept us together. Joe said to him, "Every single time you have seen Debra and me together, you have been without your wife. We don't have any secret other than that we want to be together. Instead of running around the world by ourselves, we have been enjoying life's precious moments together. We not only love each other, we like to be *with* each other."

Joe's friend said, "I guess you answered my question. I think I love my wife, but I sure don't like her. Thanks for the reality check." Duh!

Another case in point was the time we were in a club and we noticed a male friend of ours partying and having a good time with the ladies. He had had one drink too many and was really hanging loose. He came over and attempted some small talk about how he was happy to see us and how he had always admired our togetherness. He said to Joe, "Man, how do you keep it so together?"

Being together is the key to "keeping it together."

Joe and I saw an interesting episode of *Masterpiece Theater* on PBS. On the program, two male doctors shared a practice. The female nurse was attracted to one of the doctors, though both men were married. The doctors enjoyed horseback riding for recreation. The nurse overheard their conversations and she decided to take an interest in horses. One day, Doctor A and his wife were at the stable and noticed Doctor B and the nurse were riding together. A few weeks later, Doctor A and his wife were dining at a fine restaurant, where they saw Doctor B and the nurse enjoying a candlelight dinner. Doctor A and his wife were embarrassed and upset because they both knew Doctor B's wife. Doctor A didn't want his practice to be jeopardized by this affair, but he was reluctant to confront his partner.

Doctor A's wife commented that it was a shame that this beautiful young woman, who had so much potential, would waste her youth with this mature man. Her husband replied, "My dear, that is the problem with most single women. Although she is very beautiful and has a promising career, her self-esteem is not healthy. If she truly loved herself, she would invest the time to find a fine young man suitable for her. Instead, she believes that this mature man is like a horse at the stable—already broken in. Why should she spend time trying to break in a young stallion who is wild, when the other horse is broken in? As for my dear partner, Doctor B, he is too busy looking for greener grass on the other side, but soon he will discover that this greener grass is a lot tougher to chew."

Joe and I sat for several hours talking about the PBS program and the number of our friends and relatives who have split because of their cheating hearts. We thank God that we have embraced each other with love. Occasionally, friends or relatives have tried to come to our house with a "friend," but we have politely asked them to leave and not to insult us by trying to hide their duplicity in our home. If they want to cheat, they don't have to involve us.

Joe and I talked about what our marriage vows mean to us, and what it would take to keep enriching our marriage. That night we made a pledge to yearly write down and review our spiritual, family, financial, professional, and personal goals, and to reaffirm our union every five years at least.

The PBS program reminded me of friends who do things apart from their mates. They travel with groups on fabulous trips that you would think they would want to share with their partners. Sometimes you see a bunch of married women in a nightclub while their husbands are in another club across town getting their so-called groove on. On Monday morning at work, these people are the first ones to ask me how I keep my marriage alive and exciting. Duh! I feel like saying, "Should we play back the last seventy-two hours, from Friday to Sunday night, to figure this one out?"

By now you might be tired of the word *together,* but like the old song says, together we stand, divided we fall. We travel together, we play together, we do things together as a family, we conduct business together, and we go to church together. You'll never stay together if you spend all your precious time apart.

Keys to Save Your Marriage from Others

- ♥ Be faithful and worthy of trust.
- ♥ Avoid the appearance of evil, and evil itself.
- ♥ Keep the lines of communication open.
- ♥ Don't flirt and don't entertain flirting.
- ♥ Respect your spouse and give him or her honor in public.
- ♥ Keep yourself in good shape physically, emotionally, socially and spiritually.
- ♥ Do things together.

Chapter 12
Coping with Amnesia

Whoso loves—believes the impossible.

—Elizabeth Barrett Browning
Aurora Leigh, 1856

Recently I had a conversation about "perceptions" with my friend Frances Smith Dean. We were talking about how some single women think that married women have it easy, while most married women would say it's the other way around. As longtime wives, Frances and I concluded that single women don't see the dedication, energy, and hard work that goes into making a relationship work. She and I agreed that the old saying is true: Behind every good man is a good woman.

Well, to be honest, it cuts both ways. In a committed relationship, each person brings certain strengths that complement their spouse's unique qualities. Joe is strong in areas where I am weak, and vice versa. In a lot of mar-riages, these differences cause conflict. But rather than resenting what our partner doesn't do well, we should see their weakness as an opportunity to use our strength.

The root of many of our problems in marriage is the

pride we have that seeks to cover over our weaknesses. Instead of saying, "You're right, I need help with that," we get defensive and lash out. Couples discover their gifts in a relationship through constant communication, trials and tribulations, and years of experience together. We start out looking for a magic formula and end up learning how to bear each other's burdens.

In my marriage, for example, because I'm well organized and a stickler for details, I handle the family finances. But when we go out to make a major purchase, Joe's the negotiator and the objective person, so he's usually the one to work out the best deal. We have learned to acknowledge each other strengths in dealing with family matters and business issues, and we have become more adept at covering each other's weaknesses without recrimination. Joe is quite a procrastinator but I know precisely when to step into the picture. In relationships, I'm not as flexible as he is, so Joe often has to step in and smooth feathers or referee the situation.

And where is it written that both partners can't be strong in the same area? After my initial struggles in the kitchen, I did learn to cook and I prepare most of our meals. Every once in a while, Joe steps up and does some cooking. Now I suppose that I could resent him for "stepping on my turf," but I actually appreciate those times because it takes a burden off of me. Why can't we extend that same attitude to other areas? Rather than feeling crowded when our spouse tries to step up in one of our areas of strength, why don't we encourage their efforts to improve? Once again our old pride gets in the way.

Frances and I agreed that friction occurs when a spouse starts to grab the glory for their partner's success. We're not saying that wives never do this, but in our collective experience, it's the men who like to boost and brag about family accomplishments. Frances and I have seen this problem arise in dealing with teacher/student issues, credit history clean-up, managing stock portfolios, locating a day care service, choosing schools for our kids, tax and financial planning, purchasing a home or a new car, and major vacation planning. There's something about a man that causes him to get "amnesia" when everything has been handled by his wife. You hear him talking with his buddies or business associates, and all of a sudden your own blood, sweat and tears are being portrayed as your husband's brilliant idea and full responsibility. To hear a man tell the story, he's the rocket scientist who figured out what to do and the clever person who cut the deal. Seldom does his wife receive even honorable mention for her role in the decision making process.

A few years ago, I developed a plan to save for a trip to Hawaii. I established a budget and made all the arrangements with the travel agent. I cooked more meals at home to cut down our dining out expenses and I decreased our entertainment budget to make a few more dollars per week available toward our goal. But by the time we landed for our two weeks in Maui, Kauai and Oahu, Joe had come down with a bad case of "amnesia" and, as far as he could remember, our trip was his grand vacation idea.

Spousal amnesia can also be caused by parent/teacher conferences at school. Most of the mothers I know endure these meetings that are called to resolve problems with a child's classroom conduct, incomplete work, and lack of focus or lack of interest in school. Of course, when the husband tells the story later, he attributes any improvement in behavior or grades to his disciplinary action. The wife rarely receives proper credit. The hubby thinks that because he was a sounding board for his wife, he was the one who really solved the problem.

Fortunately, this kind of amnesia can often be "cured" by a gentle reminder. Many of my arguments with Joe evolve from differences over money management. All shouting aside, he and I have fundamentally different views about finances. We wrangled for years, but I could never get him to see my point of view until I finally suggested that maybe a financial planner could mediate and give us an objective opinion. Later when Joe was posturing with his friends about what a good idea it was to consult with a financial planner, I gently reminded him that it had been my idea. "Oh, yeah, you're right," he said.

I made my point in that exchange but, unfortunately, in most cases it's a short-term solution. The next chance he gets, you can bet that your husband will once again be elevating his own story with his buddies.

After about an hour of discussing how men can be, Frances and I had to laugh when we both acknowledged that we wouldn't trade places with single women for the world. I had to admit that I have never washed a car, changed the oil, put out the trash, made household repairs, or negotiated a deal for a new car. We had to give credit to our men for their many contributions to our successful lives, even if they do crowd us out from time to time. Like most wives, we cope with our husbands' "amnesia," even when it drives us insane, because any good relationship includes a mixture of qualities that offset, balance, enrich or complement each other. We take the good with the bad—it's called dealing with reality.

If there is a single message that we want to communicate, it's that every couple chooses the quality of their marriage relationship. Regardless of where you started, and no matter where you are today, you have the freedom and the ability to decide how you want your future to unfold. Exercising that freedom and developing your abilities may be the hardest thing you've ever done, but it is possible. And if you are willing to take the bad with the good and make the best of what you have to work with, you can create a beautiful marriage *together* with your spouse. Remember, don't worry about all the things you can't do, take the step you can. Start to do the little things that matter; if necessary, change your own behavior or attitude, and find ways to build up your partner. Get outside help when it's appropriate, and keep on moving toward your goals. Anchor yourself in your commitment to your spouse to stay together and to work out your marriage together.

There's also a positive form of spousal amnesia, and that's the kind that forgets the pain your partner has caused you. Too often we want to hang on to the hurts from the past, because somehow they justify our disappointment with our present situation. If we can blame our troubles on something our partner said or did, it shields us from our own responsibility to make positive changes for the future. A "good amnesia" forgets the bumps and bruises that happen along the way and focuses on making the most of each new day. Granted, it's a lot easier to "forget" when your spouse isn't causing ongoing disruption and pain, but we always have the ability to choose our response, no matter how bad the circumstances.

We recognize that many couples contend with severe problems, dire circumstances and devastating consequences. We don't mean to minimize the size of the challenges that some people face. But we do want to offer hope and encouragement.

Keys to Save Your Marriage from "Amnesia"

♥ Choose to have a good marriage, full of fun and good feelings.

♥ Brag about your spouse, not about yourself.

♥ Remain open-minded. Don't run a racket on your spouse.

♥ Give your partner credit for his or her strengths.

♥ Learn to compliment each other.

♥ Always consider your spouse's opinion.

♥ Sometimes having to answer questions or justify your decisions helps you to think through your own viewpoint more completely.

♥ Take the time to teach your spouse in areas where you are strong.

♥ Make tomorrow better than today.

Chapter 13

Interdependent Independence

Many waters cannot quench love, neither can
floods drown it.

—Song of Solomon 8:7

One day in 1980, I sat Debra down and said, "What would you do if something happened to me?" She didn't have an answer. Later, when I asked her again, she told me she was still pondering the question.

"Wrong answer!" I said. "When we first met and were dating, you would have responded in a heartbeat. You would have said, 'I'd just do without.'"

When Debra was younger, she was never at a loss for words. I always loved her quick wit and her ability to think on her feet. She was always armed and ready to tell me her opinion and her expectations. So for Debra not to be ready to answer my question was cause for concern. Her ability to follow through quickly with precise, detailed, logical and organized thoughts seemed dampened.

As a result of my question, we started one of the most significant conversations we have ever had in our marriage. We both understood that we needed to think about the future beyond our relationship, and Debra was quick to realize that we needed a plan.

Throughout this book we have been discussing the importance of doing things together in a marriage, but it is also important to create a plan for what to do if your spouse dies or is disabled. Nobody wants to think about such possibilities, but you're foolish if you don't. Over the course of our twenty-three years together, Debra has become very dependent on my input on all important matters. Of course, that is entirely appropriate since I'm her husband. But no loving husband would want his wife to be so dependent that she would struggle mightily to get by if he were no longer on the scene.

I could see the lightbulb go on in Debra's head when she realized that in a lot of ways she had stopped trusting her own instincts. In marriage we want to be inter-dependent without becoming co-dependent. A co-dependent partner is weakened by his or her overreliance on the other person. When a couple is interdependent, they work together to maximize their collective strengths and minimize their weaknesses, and both partners grow stronger in the process. Don't allow yourself or your spouse to go soft just because right now you are meeting each other's needs. If *you* stay sharp, your relationship stays sharp.

After I had been out of school for a couple of years, a friend of mine called one day and told me to drop by the gym at Xavier University, where an NBA scout would give me a look-see. I had been focused on getting my career underway and was only playing basketball occasionally, so I wasn't in peak condition, but I decided to show up at the gym anyway. When I arrived, it was obvious which guys had been lifting weights, shooting hoops and working out. We played three-on-three full court and I did fine for about the first five minutes. Then my lack of tip-top conditioning caught up to me and I began to fade. I had already figured out that my future wasn't in the NBA, which was why I was off doing something else, but my point is that you must be prepared for the things that are important. Most of the other guys who were in the Xavier gym that day didn't end up in the NBA either, but those who had placed a priority on basketball were as ready for their chance as they could be. You never know what life will dole out, but if you are prepared for what is important, then you are equipped to make the best of any situation.

One of the skills that I bring to my marriage with Debra is the ability to create paradigm shifts in our relationship. I challenge her to look at things in new and sometimes unconventional ways. At the same time, she challenges me to play to win and to give it all I've got.

The same issues that you need to agree upon in order to live together in marriage are the same issues that you need to be prepared to face in the event of your spouse's death—family matters, financial matters, values, lifestyle, our spiritual awareness, and professional and personal goals.

When we reviewed our situation, we realized that everything we owned was held jointly—Debra had no independent assets. Unfortunately, our society still has such a double standard that, without a husband, Debra would have a difficult time establishing her own credit if she waited until after I was gone. We decided that she should open her own savings account and begin to build some credit in her own name.

Do you have adequate life insurance to meet your

needs if your spouse dies? Obviously, your needs change over the years, so consult a qualified professional to evaluate your situation.

If you own your own business, what would happen to your assets if you were gone? Could your spouse step in and operate your business or would it need to be sold? If you are in a partnership, could you continue if your spouse died? Is there anything to sell or is the business dependent upon your personal skills or participation in order to function? In our case, my advertising specialities business has inventory and an established clientele that could be transferred to someone else. Debra's consulting business, on the other hand, is built on her personal vision and abilities, and unless the business expanded to include other consultants, it would disappear upon Debra's death.

Make it clear to your extended family how much of their participation you would want in the event of your spouse's death. Family ties are very important in times of grief, but the death of a family member can also open the door to unwanted meddling if you haven't made your expectations clear. It is important to establish clear bound-aries that stand both before and after your death.

Debra is a strong-willed person who has contributed greatly to my life and to the life of our son. Nevertheless, I need to make it clear to my family that if something should happen to me, life will go on for Debra and she will be capable of making her own decisions without their interference. In particular, I don't want them to be tampering with finances or jumping in with their opinions about how Joseph should be raised. We have been careful to establish boundaries around our personal, professional and financial lives—and, by design, our families have not been a part of that process—and after my

death is no time for them to start being involved. In order
to prepare for that possibility, Debra and I must devise a
clear plan for how she will continue if I should die first,
and vice versa. The same overall issues would apply to me
if Debra were to die, but in our society a man has an easier
time maintaining his financial and professional goals.

Debra and I witnessed the impact of an untimely
death in the life of one of our dearest friends, Wanda
Celestine. Her husband, Beverly, and I had known each
other since 1957 and he was one of my closest buddies
growing up. Beverly and Wanda were married the month
before Debra and I, so as couples we kind of grew up
together as well, and Debra and Wanda became close
friends.

Wanda faithfully stood by Beverly as he battled
cancer—rejoicing when he went into remission, and
grieving when he finally succumbed on September 12,
1994. She loved him dearly and made many sacrifices
during his illness.

Wanda took Debra and me into her confidence
during the months leading up to Beverly's death, which
gave us an inside view of some of the issues she faced.
After Beverly was gone, Wanda encouraged us to give
some thought to the "what ifs" in our own relationship.

I encouraged Wanda to move on with her life as
soon as she could and, as it happened, she met a wonderful
man within a year and they began to enjoy a new life
together. Wanda found happiness and peace in the midst of
tragedy. It is wonderful to see fulfillment, growth, and new
developments unfolding in her life. Her new man has
stepped into the positive male role and has helped her
support her young adult daughter and young son. He has
loved, nurtured and bonded with the family and has

brought new life out of a very painful experience. Wanda deserves the best of what life can offer.

Debra and I saw the pain that she endured in coming to grips with Beverly's death and the adjustments she had to make, and we decided that we needed to discuss our own relationship and make preparations for our own possible future. As much as we didn't want to face these challenges, we couldn't ignore the lessons from Wanda's experience.

Nobody wants to die or have their spouse die, but it is important to work out these details "just in case." Of course you would grieve if you lost your spouse, and of course you would face some difficult adjustments, but every couple should set as a goal how to "get on with life."

The time to talk about these sensitive topics is when your communication with your spouse is good. I caught Debra's attention in a way I hadn't anticipated when I told her that if she died I wouldn't grieve for a year or dress in black or look and act depressed every time someone asked me, "Do you ever miss Debra." I would forever miss Debra, and I would give a tactful response, but life would go on.

In response, Debra had a few choice words for me that I had never heard from her before. Maybe I wasn't as tactful as I thought I was, but the point is to come to an understanding with one another that clearly spells out your desires and intentions for how to handle all the important issues that surround the death of a loved one. Widows and widowers will often say things like, "So-and-so would have wanted it this way." The only way to know how "so-and-so" would have wanted something is to have had the conversation before he or she died.

We also discussed what would happen to Joseph if both of us were to die in an accident. Now that Joseph is older, we have talked to him about how we have tried to look ahead to protect his best interests. We have arranged for guardians until Joseph comes of age and we have made arrangements with our CPA, financial planner, lawyers, and executors so that each one knows specifically what to do in the event of our deaths. Of course, you never consider everything, but we have made the best plans we can.

Debra and I decided that the best thing we could do for each other is to love each other and to appreciate the life we have together while we're both living. We hope and pray that both of us will live long and well, but even if one of us should die prematurely, we want to live each day until then in such a way that the surviving partner can look back on a life filled with love, respect, trust, abundance, joy, peace, prosperity, happiness and fun. When I'm gone, it won't matter who comes after me, because I can only appreciate the life we shared together here and now. Even our son recognizes the powerful relationship that Debra and I share, and he would want us to be happy and fulfilled in life.

At first, Debra struggled with the idea that I would carry on after her death, but after she thought about it, she decided to make our life together so rich and rewarding that I would always judge any other woman by a very high standard. She is and always will be a "tough act to follow."

Keys to Save Your Spouse
When You're Gone

♥ Develop a clear plan for handling finances,
   children, family, and business in the event of
   an early death.

♥ Document your agreement in a will or trust
   to protect your spouse, your children and
   your assets.
♥ Encourage your partner to grieve and then
   "get on with life."
♥ Love your spouse while you still can. Make
   every day count.
♥ Equip your spouse in important areas where
   he or she is weak—especially finances, home
   management and caring for children.

Chapter 14

The Honor Roll

In matrimony, to hesitate is sometimes to be saved.

—Samuel Butler
Higgledy-Piggledy Notebooks,
1912

When a person talks about his or her spouse, often all you hear are negative comments and put-downs. Some people I've met seem willing to say almost anything about their spouse except something nice. I always had a great relationship with my father, grandfather, and seven brothers, so my image of men has always been positive. My years with Joe have been filled with love and respect for each other. Like any other couple, of course, Joe and I have had difficult times in our relationship, but I have made it a practice to uplift Joe in my thoughts and to say only positive things when I talk about him. I find myself spending less time around women who say terrible and horrible things about their mates. Listening to them carry on about everything they don't like is a useless waste of energy.

You've heard it said that you reap what you sow. That principle is never more true than in relationships. I firmly believe that the words we say about our partners create the reality we experience. Negative talk leads to negative outcomes, but if we talk positively, we will get positive results. If you are in the habit of talking trash about your spouse and you suddenly change, your friends might say, "Who are you talking about, girl?" But if your husband hears you building up his positive qualities and praising him to your friends—and if he knows that you talk like this even when he's not around—he will be motivated to develop his positive characteristics in order to live up to what you have said. The same principle applies to praising your children. People naturally rise or fall to the level of expectations that others have for them or that they have for themselves. Sow positive seeds and you will reap a positive harvest. And even tiny seeds can grow into lush and leafy plants with beautiful blossoms.

There's no magic formula for staying together, other than the conscious daily decision to give your love away in a kind and gentle way in order to be loved in return. Staying together is built on doing unto others as you would have them do unto you, which means being good to yourself by treating others well. Our lives may be full of suffering, struggle, and pain, but through it all we hang in there. We have had to support, coach, offer a listening ear, take back something mean we said in a hurtful way. Sometimes those simple acts open the floodgates to renewal in our relationships, when we cry together, declare our faith, and affirm that our togetherness as one flesh makes a difference.

There is no such thing as a perfect relationship—at least we have yet to see one. But we recognize that our problems can only be worked out with understanding and communication with each other. Quitting would be too easy. Sticking it out together through thick and thin is so much more rewarding than throwing in the towel.

To this day, if there are problems in my relationship with Joe, we work them out. Just because he and I are not seeing eye to eye on a particular day doesn't mean I can't speak highly of him among my friends and family. And if I go to a trusted friend in confidence for support, I want that person to not only look at my viewpoint, but to coach and encourage me objectively.

Joe deserves better than to have my closest friends and parents intercede or stick their noses into our affairs. The impression I want to leave with my parents is that they did a terrific job raising their little girl to shape my life in a positive way, and that I can work out my relationship with my husband in a positive way. The only Joseph Gould Jr. that my parents will ever hear about from me is a friendly, loving, spiritual man; a family man; a good provider; a fun guy who is interesting, witty, humorous, open-minded, conscientious and God-fearing. My mother grins and embraces Joe with so much love every time she sees her son-in-law. And when she looks at me she sees a happy daughter, because I am in a healthy, loving and growing relationship.

Joe and I have been blessed to be surrounded by couples who have left a lasting impression by the simple things they have said or done. We honor our friends who have stayed together for better and for worse. We look back on many authentic and special moments with friends who have touched our lives.

To our special friends and relatives who have exemplified love and passion and have demonstrated happiness, tough love, peace, harmony, trust, respect, commitment, faith, courage and caring, we salute and celebrate you in our Honor Roll.

Honor Roll

♥ *Gilbert & Antoinette Adams*

Lou & Verna Age

Jerome & Sue Anderson

Murphy & Josephine Anderson

Walter & Ora Anderson

James & Rosetta Archie

Dr. Walter & Sylvia Barial

Thaddeus & Dwanne Biagas

Oray & Julia Boston

Charles & Andrea Brimmer

Frederick & Javetta Brogan

Fred & Linda Brown

Edwin & Merceda Burns

Ronnie & Shelia Burns

Matthew & Lynnette Causey

Beverly & Wanda Celestine

Bernie & Vivian Charbonnet

Bobby & Elaine Coleman

Silas & Shirley Connor

Merlon & Patricia Crawford

Rodney & Cynthia Crim

Leroy & Anita Crump

Joe & Betty Cummings

Thomas & Barbara Cypher

Charles & Wanda Davis

Darryl & Frances Dean

Herbert & Linda Decuir ♥

♥ *Henry & Helen Dejoie*

Lloyd & Anne Dennis

Glen & Peggy Dobbins

Rev. Andrew & Alice Douglas

Ricky & Leatrice Dupre

Theo & Meryl Duroncelet

Dow & Lisa Edwards

Herschel & Shirley Epps

Kenneth & Melba Ferdinand

Rene & Pat Fleury

Ernest & Maggie Foster

Nat & Pamela Franklin

Charlie & Eunice Gardner

Richard & Cheryl Gardner

Jack & Debra Goudeau

Eugene & Jeanne Green

Quintan & Jackie Griffin

Al & Mary Guidry

Jim & Renette Hale

LeAndrew & Donna Harris

Ray & Cathy Harris

Richard & Barbara Harris

Jim & Marcia Helton

Marvin & Wanda Henry

Chuck & Edna Herring

Dominic & Barbara Hornsby

Charles & Delores Hudson ♥

Honor Roll

♥ *Brian & Malinda Jackson*

Joe & Cheryl Jackson

Forrest & Vicky JeanPiere

Charles & Lillian Jenkins

Earl & Vanessa Johnston

Greg & Gale Jones

Herbert & Carolyn Jones

Jesse & Debra Jones

Tom & Kim Jones

Andre & Suzanne Joseph

Jimmie & Cherry Keller

Vinson & Kim Kerr

Byron & Sherlyn Lambert

Keith & Carmen LeDuff

Alex & Mary Lewis

Kevin & Nancy J. Lewis

Noah & Glendalyn Lewis

Joe & Debra Liss

Edward & Lillie Mae Madison

Edward & Viola Madison

Dr. Romell & Grace Madison

Terrence & Karen Madison

Tracy & Anita Madison

Brian & Dawn Martin

Calvin & Renette Martin

Dominic & Rosemary Martin

Dr. Robert & Beverly Matheney ♥

♥ *Robert & Barbara Mathison*

Freddie & Victorine Matthews

Chris & Loretta Mbughda

Bruce & Monique McConduit

Terry & Lois Meilleur

Don & Lydia Miller

Calhoun & Gloria Moultrie

Yusef & Jamilah Muhammed

Greg & Roseanna Pappion

Alfred & Carrie Parker

Rev. David & Gwenna Patin

Herbert & Glenda Patterson

Larry & Daisy Paul

John & Louise Pierre

Paul & Monica Pierre

Allen & Gloria Powell

James & Janet Prier

Dr. Erroll & Linda Quintal

Jefferson & Andrea Reese

Burnell & Connie Reine

Jullin & Troyonia Renthrope

Edward & Virginia Riley

Willie Craft & Sally Ann Roberts

Brian & Mary Rollins

James & Jineane Sampson

Pete & Madelyn Sanchez

Dr. Allen & Cleonie Schwartz ♥

Honor Roll

♥ *Sam & Alyse Segal*

Furnell & Valerie Severin

Alvin & Loretta Shepherd

William & Erica Sherrard

Shawn & Vida Sherrard-Hannon

Kerry & Abby Shields

James & Ada Simmons

Doug & Gayle Smart

Eddie & Deborah Smith

Leonard & Georgia Smith

Tookie & Beverly Spann

James & Sylvia Speed

Milfred & Hyacienth Stiaes

Palmer & Esperanza Sullins

Stanley & Shelia Taylor

Bryan & Mary Thomas

Vernon & Sarah Thomas

William & Katherine Thomas

Marvin & Germaine Thompson

Jerry & Claudette Tolbert

Richard & Avis Trice

Harold & Flora Villere

Harold & Georgia Villere

Bush & Janis Villery ♥

♥ *Darryl & Pam Wall*

James & Faye Wallace

Larry & Julia Ware

Brent & Troye Washington

Earl & Dorothy Washington

Herman & Gloria Washington

Tyrone & Tereska Washington

Ulysess & Autrey Washington

George & Thelma Wells

King & Helen Wells

David & Veronica White

Bruce & Cindy Wilkinson

Bruce & Pauline Williams

Leslie & Jamesetta Williams

Stanley & Seneca Williams

Tom & Betty Williams

Larry & Brenda Wilmer

Benny & Patrice Wilson

Larry & Gussie Wilson

Lloyd & Odessa Wilson

Eric & Beverly Wright

Joe Nemetz & Karen Wynne

Wallace & Myrna Young